Coolamon Girl

Dianne Lucas

Coolamon Girl

For Glenda Cloughley

Coolamon Girl
ISBN 978 1 76109 175 9
Copyright © Dianne Lucas 2021

First published 2021 by
GINNINDERRA PRESS
PO Box 3461 Port Adelaide 5015
www.ginninderrapress.com.au

Thou hast committed –
Fornication: but that was in another country,
And besides the wench is dead.

>*The Jew of Malta*, Christopher Marlowe

As a woman I have no country...
As a woman my country is the whole world.

>Virginia Woolf

Author's Note

This is my version of these events. Others will have their versions of their stories. They may be the same stories.

I have chosen to change a few names for various reasons.

I first saw the Marlowe epigraph almost fifty years ago when I was studying T.S. Eliot. He uses it as the prologue to his poem 'Portrait of a Lady', and it has stuck with me ever since. It shocked me and amused me at the same time, and said so much about our attitude to the past. I'm delighted to find a home for it in my book.

1

I can't have been much more than four, if that, when my mother first beat me.

It was a perfect summer's morning, still and silent, with the older kids in the neighbourhood off at school, the men out at work, and the women in their laundries, as they were every Monday because it was washing day. I was playing with Johnny Williamson, who lived across the road. He probably should have been at school but his ears might have been hurting him again. Sometimes he had to go to the Far West Children's Home in Sydney to get them fixed. Johnny was my brother Paul's best friend, eighteen months younger than Paul, eighteen months older than me. He called Paul 'Lukey' and Paul called him 'Willo'.

In the Williamsons' dusty backyard, chooks and weeds vied for space with the wrecks of cars and trucks. There were two dogs, Butch and Wags. Butch was as his name implies and we kept our distance, especially after he bit Narelle Jarrett when she was walking down the street to her grandmother's house. Wags was like Johnny: scruffy and sweet. Johnny stayed like that, in spite of what went on inside their house. His parents drank and fought, so much so that when Johnny grew older he swore never to touch the grog or cigarettes and he kept his word.

His mum was a rail-thin woman, weathered by years of cigarette smoking and poverty. She had a voice that pierced the quiet sleepy days of our street. You couldn't tell if it was her or their cockatoo. 'Johnny! Johnny! Get home now! Get in here!' she'd screech.

But she threw the best birthday parties. She may have had to borrow chairs from our house but the spread of sausage rolls and lollies and ice cream was abundant. She always encouraged us to eat more and she didn't care if we made too much noise or messed up the tablecloth with tomato sauce drips. Mrs Williamson didn't seem to worry about how her house looked: whether there was a hole in the fibro wall of the front veranda or if one of the steps was broken. Instead, she bought a fish tank that seemed to run the whole length of the lounge room, about six feet long at least. She invited me in to have a look at it and I was agog with amazement at its bright lights and flitting little fish: some orange, some black and white striped, some plain black. On paydays, she used to buy Johnny comics and under his bed he had a huge stack that he shared with Paul and me. I loved the Phantom because he was so handsome and mysterious and the *Archie* comics because Betty and Veronica had such fun. I wanted to be them, to be as gorgeous as they were and as good at everything from fixing cars to cooking. Being as rich and popular as Veronica would have been good, too.

On this ordinary Monday morning, before I was old enough to read comics, Johnny and I were bored. We'd run our sticks through the gutter stirring up the dust and cracking the dry mud, and we didn't know what to do next. We loitered down the dusty driveway side of our house where lone blades of grass struggled up between the car tracks and red geraniums grew wearily along the wall of our enclosed sleepout.

The sleepout was divided into two by a cupboard and Paul's bedroom was in the smaller end at the front of the house. The larger area was great for playing quoits or lino-sliding in socks. Tall built-in cupboards at the back held some of Dad's yearbooks from Yanco Agricultural High School, a botany workbook or two from Sydney University, a sailor hat and ship's pennant from his navy days, and the heavy duffle jacket he wore on frosty mornings out at the farm. There were twelve large sash windows in the sleepout, hung with sturdy leaf-patterned cotton curtains sewn by my mother.

'I always wanted a house with a lot of windows,' she explained years later. 'I used to think that the more windows you had, the richer you were.'

She was right in a way, because rich people could pay others to keep their windows clean. For her, they became a marker of drudgery, and the source of dehydration and exhaustion when she did the Christmas clean on one of the hottest days of the year and fainted, ending up in hospital.

Mum's sewing machine sat on the table under these windows. The table was richly lacquered maple, our 'best' table, and had to be treated with reverence. It was the one we carried through the embossed-glass double doors and set up in the lounge room when we had guests, which wasn't very often. We only had dinner guests when relatives were in town and then Mum would cook up her specialty: tuna mornay with cheese grilled brown on top, my favourite. The rest of the time, the table held Mum's round wicker sewing basket, the black Singer sewing machine that operated with a knee lever, a pile of mending, and her latest sewing project: underpants for one of us kids, or a dress for me perhaps.

Johnny and I dawdled along the windows.

'I know,' he said. 'Let's play you show me yours and I'll show you mine.'

'What's that?' I asked.

'We show each other our bottoms. Want to do it?'

'Okay.' I flushed. I wasn't allowed to see my brother's bottom and I always wondered what it was like.

So there Johnny and I were, right outside the windows framing Mum's sewing table, our pants at our ankles and our eyes firmly transfixed on each other's bottoms. He had more to show than I did and I was amazed at his naked skin and the floppy tube thing hanging free. We stood quietly, just looking at each other, the morning air coolly caressing my bare bottom. The occasional bird trilled, a chook cackled the arrival of an egg, and lazy dogs barked half-heartedly at each other.

My mother's work that morning included fixing a shirt for Dad that required a needle and cotton from the sewing basket. I imagine she came to the sewing table quite relaxed: the washing was on the line, the meat was ready for dinner, and the house was clean.

I wonder if I've got the cotton to match this shirt, she was probably musing.

'Do you want to touch it?' asked Johnny.

I giggled excitedly, and my fingers felt the velvety softness of usually hidden skin. At that same moment, my mother pulled the curtain along its rod to give herself more light.

'Aaarrgghhh,' she screamed, confronted by the sight of her small curly-haired daughter touching the penis of the boy from across the road.

Many years later, she told me that even though she'd had four little brothers, she'd never seen a penis until she had my brother. 'And even then,' she said, 'I felt that I shouldn't be looking at it.'

'Oh surely,' some of my friends say, 'she would have seen your father's.'

'I don't think so,' I reply. 'I reckon they only had sex three times: once for my brother, then me, and later, a miscarriage, and I'm sure they didn't leave the lights on.'

On that mellifluous summer day when she saw Johnny and me through her sparkling clean window, she roared and she bellowed. Birds flapped off their roosts in squawking consternation and the bees sipping from the geraniums buzzed in confusion.

'Dianne! You dirty girl. You disgusting children! I'll get the strap to both of you. Just you wait until I get out there.'

I heard the steel in her cries as she ran to grab the strap from the middle drawer in the kitchen, where it was always waiting, looped in hibernation until its next prey appeared. Then the front screen-door slammed, rattling the masonite bottom free of its nails, and she was outside. My hands were shaking so much it was hard to hoist my pants back up. As Mum whirled around the corner, Johnny took off, dodging her and running out the open driveway gate and across the road to the safety of his own home.

She took off after him, the strap flapping fiercely in her hand. 'Johnny Williamson! I'm going to give you what for,' she shrieked. 'You wait there,' she spat back at me, but I took off too, running out the same gate but the other way, up the street past Mrs Dean's four-room cottage with the mulberry tree where we picked leaves for our silkworms, and under Ron Lynch's sprawling loquat tree that caused me many stomach aches.

Mum, realising that I was escaping, abandoned her chase of Johnny and wheeled around to come after me. I sped round Ron's corner and hurtled past the bower blooming with roses and the magic wishing well. My mother was yelling at me to stop but I knew something big had happened. My chubby little legs ran hard. My chubby little body was one big heartbeat. I don't know where I thought I was going; my known world was only half a block.

I flung around the next corner of Ron's yard into the lane that ran behind our houses. I ran alongside Ron's paddock where, on Cracker Night, he built a huge bonfire for the entire neighbourhood and everybody came and let off crackers, except little kids like me who waved sparklers. Halfway down the lane, almost at the limits of my universe, I spied our back gate and pushed through it. The dunny, camouflaged with ivy, sat just inside the fence, so that once a week, in the early hours of the morning, the councilmen could get easy access to the pan. The toilet was just my size; I could hide there. I threw myself in the door, slamming it behind me. I heard Mum coming down the lane making strange crying noises.

I stared at the back of the door and my insides sloshed like the slush in the pan. There was no lock. There was no way I could keep my mother out. I whimpered as I backed into the corner behind the wooden seat with the crack that sometimes caught my bare leg.

*

A few days later, I was lying across my mother's knees at the kitchen table as she rubbed a thick black ointment on my back, my bottom, and the back of my legs trying to calm the purple and red welts that had erupted. All of a sudden, there was a man at the back door. It was the grocer from Iverachs' shop and he'd come to collect Mum's weekly grocery order. Next week it would be the grocer from the Co-op, because Mum tried to share our custom around. The men usually sat at the kitchen table, enjoying a hot cup of tea or Nescafé, while Mum consulted her list and reeled off the groceries she needed, checking through the cupboards to make sure nothing was forgotten. In between the business of getting the order right, they chatted about who was sick or on holidays, who had won the tennis in the night comp, or which of the old people in town needed more help.

'Grocer! Hello? Anybody home. Ah, there you are.' He'd come through the laundry and was at the screen door to the kitchen.

It was Helen's father. She was the same age as me and would become my best friend. Within a few years, I would be calling him Uncle Les. I had quite a few aunts and uncles who weren't blood relations. Maybe Mum, from the far-away fecund Whitby clan, thought I was lacking.

Mum was slow to react, possibly lulled by the smoothing motion of her hand, so there were a few heartbeats before she awkwardly pulled my pants up and my skirt down. I tried to will myself into nothingness, mortified that my shame could be seen on my skin and this man would know how bad I had been.

He didn't say anything, but his mouth set into a line when he looked at my mother and his eyes went really soft when he looked at me. He talked to me, too, not to Mum. 'Hello, sweetheart, how are you today? Have you got an order for me?'

I know he'd seen, too, because in all the years afterwards whenever Helen asked if I could stay the night, her parents always agreed. 'Sure, she can,' they'd say. 'She's our second daughter, aren't you Didee? What would you like for dinner tonight? Hat eggs?'

I loved hat eggs, the egg fried in a hole in buttered bread and the crispy cut out circle of bread sitting on top, and these were the only people who ever called me Didee, or Di.

'Hel and Di,' Helen's mother used to laugh. 'What a pair.'

Years later, when we were adults, Helen admitted she'd been jealous. 'My father really loved you. Even when you and I had a fight, he and Mum would both just go, "Oh well, she's your friend, make up with her." Sometimes I thought they liked you more than they liked me.'

I'm happy to think that somebody liked me.

That quiet summer's day, when the bees buzzed lazily around the geraniums and my little heart pumped harder than it ever had, lay buried deep in my memory for more than forty years. And I spent all those years terrified of my mother.

2

'You've been trouble from the start. I don't know what I'm going to do with you.'

This was my mother's refrain, as familiar to my ears as nursery rhymes and 'All Things Bright and Beautiful', which we sang every week at Sunday school.

Even my naming had been fraught with conflict.

'I wanted to call you Ruth,' complained Mum, 'but oh no, that was too biblical for your grandmother and Pa. And Peta? That's a boy's name, they said. You can't call her Peta. And they didn't like Denise. Oh, I tell you! Finally, I had enough and I just said, she's going to be Dianne whether you like it or not.'

I don't know if my Mama and Pa liked it but I never have, especially when it was roared at me and the second syllable teetered from a lofty height. I was one of five baby girls born in Coolamon within a year of each other who were named Dianne. Two of those girls lived in Helen's street, just one block away, and I shared my schooldays from kindergarten to Fourth Form in a class with three other Diannes. I would have loved to have a name that was just mine, one that helped me get a sense of who I was. To my family, I would always be Dianne, uninflected, formal, flattened, and dull. I would have been happy with Diana, because she had a flip in her tail at least, and she was a goddess, a goddess of the hunt, but goddesses would not have been welcome in my family and probably not in Coolamon either.

Coolamon was an in-between place, not quite flat and not quite hilly, a town plonked on the railway line between Junee and Narrandera with sheep, wheat and hay as its mainstays. It sat on the south-west tablelands between the Great Dividing Range and the Hay Plains, twenty-five miles north-west of Wagga Wagga, just outside the irrigated lushness of the more interesting Riverina with its orchards, rice farms and foreigners. Our town was named after the numerous waterholes in the area that were called Coolamon Holes because they resembled the shallow bowl-like coolamons used by the Aboriginal people to carry food, water, and sometimes babies. Not that there were any Aboriginal people around to do that when I was growing up.

It was a small town under a big sky, a two-pub town with about a thousand people in the whole shire. It was famous, once, somewhere, for its extra wide main street that lemming-like flocks of sheep could be herded through on their way to the saleyards or abattoirs, well before the woollen beasts were squashed into long semi-trailers with slatted sides. The drab brown creatures blended into the paddocks around the town with hardly a tree for shelter. I thought a barren landscape was their natural environment, dry and summer-hot, dry and winter-cold, with plenty of space to be the sheep they wanted to be, but when I went to New Zealand, many adult years later, I was astonished to see crowds of plump, white sheep browsing in paddocks so green they could have been from one of my childhood Little Golden Books, where chipmunks and bunnies frolicked without fear of bindi-eyes or cranky mothers.

I don't know who my mother expected when I was born, but, after my brother, probably another docile, quiet child. Not one who cried all night for the first six months of her life. Mum couldn't understand what was wrong with me and she was still trying to understand it five decades later when we were sipping tea together in her retirement village unit.

'Maybe you were cold?' she offered one day. 'It could be pretty frosty on the back veranda, I suppose.'

It's a bit late now, I'd thought, my face stiffening. Far too late to put another blanket on.

She was right, though: it had been cold on the back veranda. All the winters of my childhood, I skittered over its icy lino as I ran between the bathroom and the crackling open fire in the lounge room.

'Shut the door after you!' Dad would boom out from his chair next to the pedestal ashtray. 'Were you born in a bloody tent?'

The back veranda of our two-bedroom Californian bungalow in Coolamon wasn't open to the weather. Tucked in between the sleepout and the bathroom, it had fibro walls, four banks of louvre windows and four doors: one out to the backyard; one into the rear end of the sleepout; one into the bathroom with its claw-footed bath that only ever held a few inches of water because of the interminable water restrictions due to one drought or another; and the last door, the tent flap back into the toasty lounge room.

When I was ten, I was on the veranda fussing with the budgerigars that I was minding for Mr Iverach next-door and Mum was doing the ironing.

'Your bassinet was on that lowboy,' she mused, 'when you were a baby. You slept out here. Not that you did much sleeping.'

The iron hissed into the back of Dad's shirt.

'Out here? I slept out here? On the back veranda?'

A memory flashed through my mind of miniature coat hangers draped in delicate white and cream baby dresses hanging in the top of the cupboard and a little pink horse on wheels tucked between stacks of folded nappies in the compartment below. I thought of the little girl who fitted those dresses sleeping out here alone and my throat ached.

The budgie cage with Blue Boy and Jiminy Cricket ended up sitting on the same little cupboard permanently when Mr Iverach gave them to me as a thank-you present for looking after them.

'Can't I have them in my bedroom?' I pleaded. 'They might freeze to death.'

'Just put another towel over the cage,' my mother suggested. 'They'll be fine.'

Blue Boy fell off his perch one night and Mum found him, stiff and dead, in the morning. 'Just old age,' she assured me when she broke the news.

It wouldn't have entered her head that it was the cold that killed him. I guess I was lucky it didn't kill me too: I just cried.

The first time I went to Sunday school, I cried too. Sitting on a pew in my starched white dress with my legs dangling, I sobbed for the whole hour. It was in the red-brick Church of England and it was the first time I'd been thrust into the world with only my bewildered-looking brother to hold on to. It was Mum's church, over the other side of the railway line that ran through the middle of town. If you walked up past Mrs Dean's and Ron Lynch's, across Loughnan Street and down one block to the end of our street, Mimosa Street, climbed through the rusty wire fence, waded through the knee-high weeds, and balanced on the shining silver tracks as you crossed the line, you would be at the church. But we weren't allowed to do that of course. At Ron Lynch's corner, we had to trudge up the Loughnan Street slope to the main street then turn right and head down the footpath past the two banks, Curtis's stock and station agent, Slattery's newsagency, Theo's café, one of the pubs and the post office, to cross at the crossing where Mr Patterson shut the gates if a train was coming, until he slipped one day and lost both his legs. And then there was still another block to go before you were at the church. It was a long journey to an unknown land for a three-year-old.

Mama, Dad's mother, with her Scottish heritage, was a rabidly loyal Presbyterian who only went to church once a year, except for funerals, and she was not happy that Mum and Dad were married in St John's Church of England in Wagga. Religious rivalry and wars were usually between Catholics and Protestants, but, for Mama, it was Presbyterians against everyone else. She smirked like she'd won an argument when I didn't cry at the Presbyterian Sunday school. It may have been because I inherited her Scottish streak but it could also be because the Presbyterian church was only about a hundred yards from our house, diagonally across the unkempt paddock on the corner opposite Ron Lynch's. Mum, the only adult in the family who ever went to church, eventually relented and went to the Presbyterian church too. It was much closer for her to rush home and turn the Sunday roast.

It was a relief to both my mother and me when I could finally go to school. No more wailing because I stubbed my toe on the raised lip of the rough concrete on the front veranda; no more playing under my mother's skirt as she tried to move around the kitchen. For her, no more having to be constantly alert for dirty hands, messy clothes, and a daughter she couldn't keep up with, so she said.

'You've always been a bull at a gate. You were running before you could walk. I heard footsteps pottering down the hall and it was you. Always wanting to read, to know everything. I couldn't wait to get you out of my hair and into school.'

I loved my new school uniform. It was winter so I wore my navy-blue tunic with the box pleats, a sky-blue shirt, and a navy tie that Mum had fixed into a permanent knot. She joined it to a piece of elastic that fitted over my head and around my neck; one less job for her to do every morning, but I wanted a tie like all the other girls, one that came loose sometimes and needed skill to retie. I wore long navy-blue socks with elastic garters, shiny black lace-up shoes, and a blue bow in my hair, but best of all, Mum had knitted me a cosy cardigan. As I walked through the front gates of the school with my new brown school port, which ended its days as the shoe-cleaning box, I felt smug and proud.

The other girls, who had started kindergarten at the beginning of the year and were already flinging their arms around each other, laughed at me. They laughed at Deirdre Hamilton too, who started the same day as me, halfway through the year, close to our fifth birthdays. They jeered because we both wore cardigans our mothers had knitted. Their cardigans and jumpers had been bought from a shop. Deirdre and I had never met before, but we gravitated towards each other and joined the parade of little girls, walking in twos or threes, around and around the infants' playground. We meandered past the concrete shelter of bubblers, where one side was for boys and the other side for girls; past the trees ringed by benches (where in the not too distant future another Deirdre from first class would sit on my lunch and squash my banana); and past the woodwork room where the big boys learnt to measure and hammer and girls weren't allowed. Around and around we went, being pointed at and whispered about, our arms flung around each other's necks. As well as a bought cardigan, it was important to have someone's neck to throw your arm around.

3

Because Coolamon was my world, I always assumed that it was my mother's world as well but, unlike most of the parents of the kids I went to school with, Mum wasn't from Coolamon and she didn't have anyone's neck to throw her arm around.

Mum was from Rocky Hall, a small hamlet in the shadow of Big Jack Mountain near Bombala on the south-east coast of New South Wales. Dairy country, not wheat and sheep. In Rocky Hall, she was surrounded by a large extended Whitby clan and was the sixth child of ten, the youngest of the four daughters. As a child, I didn't even know all my Whitby aunts, uncles and cousins, and I was oblivious to, and uninterested in, what my mother's childhood had been like. Yes, I knew that the family had cows and that the children walked miles to school barefoot and herded the cows home afterwards, picking up kindling for the fire as they went, and that was about it. I knew that Grandfather Whitby had left the farm and was working as a security guard at Parliament House in Canberra, something I used to brag about to my friends: he might as well have been the prime minister.

It wasn't until I was in my thirties that I started hounding my mother and her siblings for more information. I learnt that the dairy farm was a small holding carved out of a larger Whitby family farm, that Grandfather also grew carrots and potatoes and stored them in holes in the ground over winter, and my uncles trapped rabbits for the meat as well as their skins. Life was pretty tough at Fairy Bower, the little cottage that bulged with children during the Depression years, and everyone had to do their bit.

'Your mother was just a working girl,' Aunty Winnie, Mum's eldest sister, told me. Winnie was still resentful of her childhood into her nineties and was always very sparing with information no matter how much I pumped. Her voice would flare with indignation. 'Oh, what do you want to talk about that for?'

'They should have stopped at Audry,' she muttered one day.

'Audry's for the house. That's what Mother said,' she told me another time. 'The rest of us had to help Dad in the dairy.'

'Not when you were really little, surely?' I pressed.

'Yes, of course,' she scoffed. 'Your mother was standing on a stool mixing cakes and bread and doing the washing up when she was four. Us older kids would be out with Dad seeing to the cows or getting the garden beds ready. We'd see this little blonde head popping over the hill carting billies of tea and biscuits for us. She worked hard, your mother. We all did.'

I've always found it difficult to believe that my mother was ever a child, and especially a blonde one. That was just ridiculous. For as long as I knew her, she had black, black hair, even into her eighties. And never dyed, of course. She would be aghast if anyone even suggested it. Only women with loose morals dyed their hair. Hers was naturally black, and she was beautiful, the most beautiful one in our family.

'Some people used to think I was Spanish,' she told me, laughing. 'They'd ask if I could do the flamenco.'

I have used a magnifying glass to search the tiny two-by-three inch black and white photos of my mother's childhood, trying to recognise her amongst the gang of children. By a process of elimination, she's the one who's always scowling. Scrunched down in the grass outside the chook yard, perched on the side of a hill looking for mushrooms with the other children, or sitting for family shots with one or other of her parents, my mother is always glowering at the camera. I mightn't ever recognise her as the child with the fair hair but I came to know that scowl very well.

Mum didn't start school until she was seven, because she had to help look after the four little boys: Laurie, who always carried a dustpan brush with him wherever he went, banging whatever was in sight; the twins, John and Keith; and Garnet, the baby.

'There was many a time I wanted to push the pram with one of them in it off the veranda,' she told me. 'And I did it once. The day Laurie whacked the beehive and the bees stung him all over. He'd been told not to, and I was the one who had to look after him. He wouldn't stop crying, carrying on, and I got so fed up I just tipped him over the edge. Grandmother Whitby was not happy.'

Mum had to leave school when she was thirteen to help her mother again, this time in the cake shop. It was 1940, the early years of the Second World War, and Grandmother Whitby had packed up the sulky with Mum and the younger boys and left Fairy Bower for good. She took them up the mountain to Queanbeyan, where she whipped a lice-and-flea-infested shack into shape and opened a cake shop that supplied the army, navy and air force canteens in Canberra. Grandmother chose to do that rather than live another day in the same house as her husband without contraception and with his unfulfilled promises of electric lights and running water. The Towamba River that lapped the back door of their cottage when it was in flood didn't count.

My mother never spoke about having friends in Queanbeyan. The only friend I ever knew about was Denise, who became her bridesmaid and one of my godmothers, but they had met after Mum left home and was working in the post office in Griffith, further along the railway line from Coolamon. Griffith was where my mother and father had met too. Ross was the knight in shining armour who rescued young Audry from her fiancé, Jack, and from Jack's parents.

'You were engaged before Dad?' I asked stunned. 'Who was he? What happened to him?'

'He was a schizophrenic, or maybe it was lead poisoning from being a house painter,' she mused. 'He turned very nasty. Aggressive. We met in Canberra and got engaged and when he moved to Griffith to be closer to his parents, I applied for a transfer and was able to follow him. I even lived at his parents' house. It wasn't long before he started drinking a lot and made life a nightmare. His parents blamed me and I didn't even drink.'

'Well, what happened?' I persisted. 'How did you get out of it?'

'Oh, one Saturday afternoon they sent me to fetch him home from the pub and he called me all sorts of names, I can't even tell you. He kept it up all the way home. I'd had enough, so I packed my bags and left. His father called me all sorts of names then too, names I'd never heard before. Good riddance to bad rubbish, I say.'

'And Dad? Where was he?'

'I went to stay with Denise and he lived in the same boarding house. That's where I ended up staying. There was a whole mob of us and gosh we had fun. Playing tennis, going swimming, going to dances. But Jack kept pestering me. He'd come into the post office and grab at me across the counter. I was quite scared. I thought he might come in with a gun and shoot me. He came to the boarding house one night when I was there alone. He was drunk, as usual. I told him to go, that it was definitely over, and to leave me alone. I'd been playing Patience and he up-ended the card table and pushed me against the wall. Your father came in at that moment and kicked him out. I don't know what he said but Jack never bothered me again.

I don't know if my father already had his eye on Mum, his good eye, but it was his bad eye that really brought them together. When Dad was at school at Yanco Ag, sent there from Coolamon as a boarder from the age of twelve, a piece of metal had flown into his eye. Then, when he was in the navy during the war, his eye ulcerated. It could have been the Pacific heat and humidity or the stress of being on the only minelaying vessel in the south-west Pacific, hoping the safety devices on the mines sent to hang in the depths every eleven seconds were working properly. He never talked about the war, except to say that he hated the Yanks and their tailor-made smokes. He was demobilised because of corneal scarring and, when I was a child, he used to go to Concord Hospital in Sydney for a few weeks at a time. He always came home with the toys out of the cornflakes packet and a patch over his eye. I was scared of the patch – he looked like a pirate – so Mum made little eye patches for Paul and me to wear. I later learned that my father had the first corneal transplant in Australia and he was a medical success story. A photo of his eyes was in the *Daily Telegraph* and there was another photo of him reading a newspaper.

In Griffith, well before the transplant, his eye had ulcerated again: this time when he was doing crop research with the CSIRO. Mum had leapt to his aid and did all his ironing. For the rest of her life, she kept a folded-up square of once-rumpled brown wrapping paper which had a slip of white writing-paper sticky-taped to it. 'Dear Audry,' it said. 'Thanks for being such a sweet kid. Bundles of love, Ross xxx.' Mum was smitten, but, unfortunately for her, that was to be the romantic highlight of their forty-year marriage.

'Your father only married me because of your grandmother,' she told me. 'She pressured him into it, I'm sure. When he moved back to Coolamon from Griffith, he nagged me to put in for a transfer to the Wagga post office, so I did, and every Friday night he'd come in and pick me up and take me to Coolamon for the weekend. Trouble was, he'd drop me at his parents' place and then go off with his father to the pub. Same thing on Saturday and Sunday: I was left with Mama while he and Pa went to the football or the Bowling Club. I think your grandmother knew that if she left it up to your father, he'd never settle down at all. He was only interested in one thing and that was the grog. And I was stupid enough to say yes. I should've known better.'

My mother, who hated both drinking and smoking, really did pick the wrong family to marry into. I grew up thinking houses that didn't have beer in their fridge were strange. It was as much a part of Lucas family life as sleeping and eating. Beer had already thickened my father's girth in their wedding photos and it's always been hard to recognise him in the earlier photos of the long, lean, almost feminine-looking young lad with flawless fresh skin and full lips. I recognise him by his eyes, the palest shining-blue eyes I've ever seen.

Sometimes when Dad and Pa had a skinful, I thought they were the funniest and cleverest men in the world and my belly muscles would ache from laughing. Those times became fewer and fewer as the years passed and, instead of laughter at Mama's tea table, there would be tension and silence as the men with the bulging bellies snarled about everyone and everything.

The biggest drinking day of the year in Coolamon was, of course, Anzac Day, and every year my father and grandfather donned their best suits, pinned on their medals, and joined the other men to march down the main street. Dad was often the sergeant, 'ten-hutting' them into formation in the awful silence that enclosed the town, a silence that was broken only by the sound of boots advancing on the cenotaph where their own names were carved in stone alongside the names of the men who never came back, or who, like Pa's brother George, did come back but died from tuberculosis picked up in a foreign land.

We kids marched too, the first outing of our winter school uniforms for the year, complete with gloves and berets and rosemary pinned to our blazers. April could still be hot, though, and more often than not people fainted, even Scouts and some of the soldiers who came over from the army base in Wagga. After the ceremony, the men retired to the RSL Hall, where Mama and the other women served them a hot dinner before leaving them to the grog and their memories.

I was very proud that Pa had a medal from fighting at Gallipoli, and I knew he'd been in France because he tried out French words on me when I started learning it at school. To make the trifecta, he'd fought in Egypt too, but I never knew, until I was an adult, years after he died, that he had been buried alive in a bomb crater at Gallipoli and had nightmares about it for the rest of his life. No wonder he drank.

'Your Pa sure could drink,' people have said to me.

'Your father liked his drink too, that's for sure,' they'd laugh.

I have wondered if it was the grog that stopped my father graduating from university after he left the navy, and ultimately brought him back to Coolamon, the farm, and Lucas family expectations.

Those expectations started with my Lucas great-grandfather, who arrived in Coolamon with his family in the 1870s, when he was fourteen. There were so many Lucases around when I was growing up that we hardly even called ourselves cousins. My grandmother's mother, Nan Baird – or Eugenie Alice Dyce as she was then – had travelled to Coolamon from Gundaroo in the 1880s in a horse and cart with her parents and their chooks. Nan Baird, and her two younger brothers, my great-great uncles, were part of my childhood life too: Uncle Colin was an elder at our church, and Uncle Lin lived opposite the swimming pool. I went to school with all their Dyce grandchildren, and we didn't call each other cousins either.

My father's family and its history engulfed my mother, and none of her own family were within cooee. The closest was in Canberra, a four-hour drive in those days, so it might have been another world. Once she was married, Mum couldn't work in the post office any more because of the government marriage bar against married women working in the Public Service, so she started helping out with Dad's trucking business. Dad liked to work from the front bar of the pub, so she often found herself alone at work as well as at home.

'When I was pregnant with your brother, I got fed up with it,' she told me. So she shut the door of the office and went home to her lovely cottage with its shady front veranda, standard roses in the middle of the lawn, and chook yards out the back.

'Your grandparents turned up on the warpath,' she said. 'They both had a go at me. Said I was disloyal. That I was getting too big for my boots. Who did I think I was to make the decision to shut the office? On and on they went. But I stuck to my guns. I'd had enough. In the end, your father couldn't keep the business going by himself, so he went to work on the family farm, and that was that. They always blamed me. Never hesitated in telling me what I was doing wrong.'

The Lucases had expectations of this woman who had married their eldest son: she shouldn't just obey her husband but she should join the local Country Women's Association and follow in the footsteps of Nan Baird, who had been Coolamon's inaugural president, and Mama who, along with all the Lucas women, had stints as president, secretary and treasurer. She was also expected to uphold the honour of the Lucas family and to keep up the fiction of the Lucas squattocracy, which gave Mama her credibility as a matriarch of the town. Status in Coolamon came from how much land you had, how well off your family had been, and how much you could borrow from the bank. Mum had to pretend that the farm was a going concern, that the Lucas coffers had not been depleted, and that Dad and Pa were not drinking the farm away.

Not that Mama ever seemed to worry about their drinking. For all her airs, she had a great tolerance, even a fondness, for drunks. 'Poor chappie,' she'd say.

Mum couldn't understand it. 'It's not as if she's had an easy time of it, that's for sure,' she told me. 'He could be an old devil, your grandfather, and nasty sometimes too. I thought he was going to hit her the day your Aunty Marg was getting married. Pa wanted to go to the pub before the service but your grandmother knew he'd just get too sozzled to walk Marg down the aisle. She wasn't taking any chances, so she hid all his trousers. You should have heard him! I don't know why she put up with it.'

I don't know why my mother did either.

With no one's neck to throw her arm around, and parents-in-law perched ready to swoop, my mother was lonely in those first years of her marriage. She eventually made friends with other outsiders: postmasters' wives, until their husbands were posted to a new address, or the wives of men arriving to fill a gap in the council for a year or two. She didn't lounge in houses she'd grown up in or gossip and laugh with cousins and old school friends. There was nobody who had known her when she rode her bike delivering cakes; there was nobody who had been her ally or confidante when she had arguments with her mother. In Coolamon, they only knew her as Ross's prim and fussy wife.

Women are often the ones who hold the cultural knowledge and memory of a community or a family. They learn it at their mother's knee. My mother's cultural knowledge came on a dairy farm at the base of a mountain more than a day's drive away from the tablelands of Coolamon, at the knee of her English war-bride mother, when Grandmother stopped working long enough to sit down. She learnt to bake and stew and preserve and sew and knit and crochet, and she learnt about scrimping and saving and making do. She saved string, rubber bands, brown paper, plastic bags, paper bags, jars, bottles, and alfoil, well before the word recycling was invented; she encouraged Paul and me to collect newspapers and sell them to the butcher; margarine could do instead of butter and the wrappers were kept for lining cake tins; if the hens weren't laying, milk was as good as eggs for breadcrumbing fish or lamb's brains; and over summer, any spare eggs were rubbed with a preserving cream and stored in the dark cool fireplace for winter cooking. Every possible part of a killed sheep or pig was used: tongues, stomachs and pigs' trotters. My mother learnt all these things but she didn't learn about larking about and having sleepovers with friends. No wonder Coolamon-bred women thought she was uptight.

4

Mum was never a Bex-and-a-good-lie-down sort of person – she preferred to rub her temples with Dencorub – but for what seemed like a very long time she was more in bed than out of it.

She was in bed on my eighth birthday and I was allowed to bring my new red Malvern Star bike with its basket and elastic skirt protectors into the bedroom to show her. Dad said it had fallen off the back of a truck but, thankfully, it wasn't damaged. At last, I had my own wheels. When I was younger, we'd borrowed a three-wheeler trike from Malcolm Campbell, who lived at the end of our street in a house with peacocks on the front screen door. All the women said it was bad luck to have peacocks on your front door and they may have been right because Mr Campbell ran off with someone else and the father of the family who lived there next became sick and died. The peacocks were still there when Ivan Moses moved in with his wife and kids, and he died too, a hero fighting a bushfire. Two elderly sisters moved in next and removed the peacocks and nothing happened after that. I sometimes wondered what was in the wrong place at our house that had made my mother sick.

She was in bed, too, when our first television set was delivered. After it came, we never played tiddlywinks, pick-up-sticks or Chinese Chequers before bed any more, and Mum and Dad didn't listen to *Dexter* on the wireless on Tuesday nights or *The CIB* on Wednesday nights. Instead of the occasional murmur of conversation, I went to sleep with the staccato voices and mood music from *The Naked City*, *Perry Mason* and *Homicide*.

And she was in bed the day a tornado twisted through our town making *Leave It To Beaver* all snowy. Paul and I had huddled in the bedroom with her while the whirlwind flung the tangle of scrub bordering our streets into even more confusion. It lifted corrugated-iron roofs and carried them across the railway line; it picked up toys from backyards and redistributed them willy-nilly. I didn't know which was more terrifying, the roaring wind or my mother barely able to raise her head.

The day came when she was moved to the hospital, a grand old white homestead with a shady veranda and a wide linoed hall. When I walked in its over-large front door, strange smells assailed me: disinfectants and sickness. I hoped I didn't catch anything by breathing them in.

A couple of days later, I was standing outside the hospital fence watching as they wheeled my mother out on a stretcher and put her in an ambulance to take her to a bigger hospital in Wagga. She probably didn't care that the small crowd gathered were seeing her in her home-made dressing gown, a dark maroon corduroy that set off the stark paleness of her face. The only other time she hadn't cared what the neighbours might think was when dogs from down the back lane had killed all her baby chickens at four o'clock in the morning. She charged down the lane to confront the owner with only her nightie on.

There were quiet murmurs as her stretcher passed.

'Bye Audry. I'll be thinking of you.'

'See you, Audry. Come back soon.'

I wondered if, like me, everyone else was scared she was going to die.

I didn't know much about death. My great-great-uncle Colin was the only person I'd known who'd died. I was seven and asleep in bed when Jim, Dad's cousin and best friend, came knocking urgently at the door in the early hours of the morning to fetch Dad because Uncle Colin and his wife Ethel had been killed in a car accident driving home from a footy match in Wagga. I heard the shock and low rumble of sadness in the men's voices, the tears in my mother's. I heard Dad go with Jim (to identify the bodies, I found out years later) and I knew something bad had happened.

'Just go back to sleep,' urged Mum when I called her in. 'It'll be morning soon.'

Next morning, she sat on the edge of my bed and told me what had happened. I felt the soft flutter of death at the base of my throat as my breath stopped briefly to mark the passing. It was just a small hiccup in my life, but it's when I started my collection of people I would miss.

I've always reckoned you would be best off dying in a town like Coolamon, especially as it was when I was growing up. It would be even better if you were Catholic or Church of England because those funeral services were held in the churches on the other side of the railway line and the hearse had to lead the cortege at a turtle pace up the main street to get to the cemetery down our end of the town. All the shops would shut their doors and the shopkeepers and shoppers would stand alone or gathered in clusters under the wide veranda roofs along the footpath, the men holding their hats in their hands or to their hearts, and the women, shopping baskets resting at their feet, holding their children still. Except for the odd holey muffler, silence would engulf the tableau, until the last car slipped out of sight. Then, with a collective sigh, movement resumed, but in a more subdued fashion.

For a while after Uncle Colin died, as I was going to sleep, I imagined both my parents dying and leaving me alone in the world. My heartbeat quickened with terror and the murmur of voices from the lounge room provided no comfort: the night seemed too dark and the world too big. Sobs would come and I'd have trouble getting my breath. I felt like my head might explode at any moment and I'd grope my way into the lounge room, startling my parents, but without words to tell them what was wrong. I'd just sob and Dad would sit me on his knee in front of the fire and hold me until I calmed down, the smoke from his cigarette wafting over my head and up the chimney.

'There, there, Chicken, you'll be all right. It'll all be okay.'

I didn't know if it would be okay when Mum was in hospital. All I knew was that she was really, really sick, so sick that she was in a Catholic hospital, closer to God I expected. The few times I visited her in the two months she was there, it was so quiet, so still, and she was so pale and weak, I hardly dared speak.

When they took her away, Paul and I and Lassie, our little fox terrier, were moved to Mama and Pa's. Their house was over the other side of the railway line from ours, a block up the hill from the railway, on the corner of a crossroads and diagonally opposite the hospital. The Shire Chambers was on another corner, and Pa's brother, Uncle Perce's house was on the other. When Mama and Pa moved into town from 'Old Springfield', the family farm, this house had been a strategic purchase: it wasn't just a sign that the family was of an elevated social standing, but, more significantly, Pa could get a skinful at the pub down on the bottom corner opposite the railway and find his way home just by keeping one foot in the gutter.

I loved their house; it was my second home. Paul and I stayed there whenever Mum and Dad went out to a ball dressed in their finery, or for no special reason at all. The first photo of me was taken on its front veranda and I grew from being a little girl scared of falling through the sheep grid in the driveway to striding across it. The house had a bullnose veranda around three sides with a deeper veranda at the back. The walls were twelve-inch-thick mud brick, some with long cracks running through. When nobody was watching, I liked rubbing the grainy dried mud free. In the backyard, the Hills hoist had a permanent warp from when our aunties, Marg and Gene, swung us around. Inside, the house was cool and dark. All of us who grew up there knew which side of the hall to avoid so the creaks wouldn't wake my grandmother. It was safest close to the pegboard that had lots of framed photos of Paul and me and our cousins, as well as a china swan, an ashtray with an Aboriginal man with a spear balancing on one leg, and a collection of paperbark pictures all made by Mama. Mama could make anything. She tanned sheep hides into the fluffy, soft rugs in front of the fire that Lassie and I fought over; she mosaiced wine flagons and turned them into lamps; and she converted the blue velvet dress I wore to Aunty Marg's Coolamon wedding into a Little Bo Peep costume, complete with frilly petticoats. She even made me a golden crook.

My evening lullaby at Mama and Pa's was the grinding down of gears as the trucks lumbered up the slope to Wagga. Tucked up in Mama's high squishy double bed in the front room (after she had decamped to one of the twin beds in the girls' room), I could imagine myself being a grown-up. So, too, when I smoothed my hands over the brown, velvety upholstery in the formal lounge room as I hosted pretend tea parties, and when I twirled the phone cord in my fingers as I sat at the telephone table in the hall with the heavy bakelite phone held to my ear, chatting to nobody.

Staying for the months my mother was away, though, didn't feel quite so comforting.

Mama took on the responsibility to make me a good girl but she didn't like girls much – except for her two daughters – or maybe it was just me she didn't like. I was her only granddaughter, so I could never test my theory. Mama doted on my seven boy cousins, and my brother was the king of them all, the first grandchild and the son of the eldest son: it doesn't get any better than that. During that time, while my father was living the life of a bachelor, Paul held court at Mama and Pa's.

Life for me went on pretty much the same except the walk to school was a bit longer, and I played with Carol next door instead of Helen. I still had to do my homework, dry the dishes, set the table, and wipe that look off my face. Paul didn't have to do anything, except his homework, and Pa helped him with that. Nearly every night, when Pa was home from the pub, the two of them played Strip Jack Naked in front of the fire, cackling and whooping as the court cards fell. I begged to play, but all my sulking, pouting and whining fell on deaf ears.

'Come and dry up, Dianne,' called Mama. 'And put that lip away, young lady. There'll be none of that here.'

It was hard to put my lip away because I had become a secret chewer. I chewed until I tasted blood, and then I chewed some more. Mama thought I just had mouth ulcers and all I needed was a pick-me-up tonic, but I did it to myself, and I made them very bad. My lips swelled with bloody sores that soon became white with dead skin. They stung and hurt when I ate or drank. The air brushing past made them ache. Talking was difficult and I couldn't shut my mouth properly. Mama painted my lips with gentian violet and I went to school with purple lips, but I couldn't stop myself. As soon as one lot healed, I started a new batch.

After the months in hospital, my mother was still alive and went to Terrigal for a two-month convalescence. I didn't see her again until she met us in Sydney for my Aunty Gene's wedding. I was more excited, though, about being a junior bridesmaid in a dusky-rose velvet frock with my hair piled up on top of my head. In the family wedding photo, Mum looks fragile and thin but she's smiling.

'What actually happened to you then?' I asked her years later. 'Was it something to do with a miscarriage?'

'No,' she replied. 'It was my ovaries. They were diseased. When I went to the doctor about the pain, he just said I was neurotic and hysterical. Ooh! I hated him. I was so frustrated I even went to an iridologist in Wagga. He said it was my ovaries. And that's what it was.'

The problem had started when my mother's bowel developed a leak, and toxic waste dripped into her pelvic cavity and onto her ovaries. She had a double oophorectomy, where both ovaries are removed, and her small intestine was resectioned, meaning they cut off a large stretch of it and her small intestine became even smaller.

'They jabbed me with so many needles,' she said, 'in my arms, my legs and my stomach, that there was nowhere to put another one.'

During the time my mother was away, Helen's father became ill too and I daydreamed that if Mum died and Uncle Les died Dad could marry Aunty Gwen and Helen and I could be sisters. I never thought about my father dying and Mum marrying again. I must have known even then that she would be happier without a man in her life.

Sometimes, I used to wish my mother had died, especially when the strap came out of the third drawer. I always seemed to be in the laundry when she discovered my crimes. I'd be cleaning my school shoes on the specially cut masonite board that fitted over the laundry tub so we didn't get polish on the floor and I'd hear the drawer slam and then she'd be at the laundry door.

'I know what you've been up to, young lady,' she'd snarl.

Sometimes I didn't know myself. I'd cringe away trying to get out of her reach wanting to disappear down the crack across the red concrete floor. Blood rushed from my face as she struck at my legs, her words punctuating the blows.

'Don't do it again. Do you hear me?'

'Yes, Mum,' I'd stutter, tears watering my silent outrage, wishing she was dead.

To ward off these evil thoughts, I added a new prayer to the five prayers I already said at night, promising I would try harder to be a good girl like she wanted so I didn't get the strap any more.

5

My brother was never bored like me. Maybe it was because he was what they called a slow learner but more likely it was because while I was drying the dishes or shelling the peas, he and Johnny were outside kicking a ball, practising their skids, or playing cricket against the garbage bin in the back yard. Occasionally, they let me play cowboys and Indians with them and I could be Lieutenant Rip Masters from *Rin Tin Tin*, but mostly I had to be his girlfriend. I was lucky I didn't have to be Rinny. One day, they finally let me choose what to play and I made them act out the *Annie Oakley* Little Golden Book, word for word. I was Annie and I got the gun, but not for long. They didn't want to play with me after that.

If I couldn't be Annie, I would happily have been Trixie Belden or Donna Parker: they solved mysteries, had adventures, and were never in serious trouble with their parents. When I was thirteen and Mr Iverach lent me his heavy old typewriter with the dodgy e key and the faded black ribbon, I started to write a novel about a girl just like Donna and Trixie, except this girl had a multitude of brothers and sisters, older and younger, so there was always someone looking out for her, playing with her, or looking up to her. She was as smart as my storybook heroines; she could throw balls straight and catch them too; and she was allowed to climb trees.

I dumped Donna and Trixie when I met Norah of Billabong. She was Australian, and she didn't have a mother who made her dust the mantelpiece or iron the tea towels and hankies. She only had a father and a brother, and they let her help with the musters and get dirty and sweaty like them. I wanted to be a farm girl like her: I wanted to wear jeans and boots; I wanted to drive myself to the farm gate to catch the bus to school; and I wanted to ride a horse. I pleaded with my mother from the darkness of my bedroom to be able to get a horse, but that stopped after I was bucked off by a friend's Shetland pony.

I always used the cover of night to make my pleas because it hid the desperation and disappointment on my face, be it when I wanted a horse, or as a teenager, when I wanted to wear a bra or to shave under my arms. Mum said then that I should wait until I had breasts or hair. I used a different tactic when I wanted to wear stockings: I wrote a long three-page pleading letter. She relented that time and I skipped up the street to buy some to wear to the school fete that night. Unfortunately, there were no step-ins in my size to hold up stockings, only the tight suffocating corsets women my mother's age wore, so Mum made two bands of elastic to go around my upper thighs instead. I felt so grown up with my silky legs except I spent the night hitching up the wrinkles at my ankles and knees.

Norah wouldn't have worn stockings but I could still have been her because we had a farm too, a thousand acres eight miles out of town, but, instead, I watched from the veranda, broom in hand, as Paul climbed into the truck with Dad or clambered into Pa's ute and went off to tend the sheep or the crops. Sometimes when he was gone, I even had to make his bed.

It wasn't that I never went to the farm but I could count on one hand the times my grandfather let me climb into his paddock-bashed old Chevy ute. Driving through town next to him, sunk down on the springless seat, I was in heaven. Pa was never in a hurry: he slouched against the driver's door, one hand on the wheel, finger ready to be raised in greeting, while the other arm, with a cigarette held between yellow stained fingers and the hairs curling on its sun-blackened skin, rested on the open window. Intermittently, he made a great ceremony of clearing his throat and hoiking mucous out onto the road.

I pretended I was Norah when I was allowed to stand on the back of the ute pushing out feed bales to drought-weary sheep as Pa drove slowly around the bare paddocks. I loved jumping down to open and shut the gates, and I loved droving with the dogs on the rutted farm roads between paddocks.

'Get back,' Pa yelled. 'Get back, ya bloody mongrel, get over here,' and the dogs ran backwards and forwards, yipping and nipping at the sheep's heels, happy in their henchmen roles.

More often than not, though, I was confined to town and after my chores were completed, I played offsider to Helen

*

I don't remember meeting Helen. It's like she was always part of my life, but the first time she appears in our family photo album is in our kindergarten picture. She was one of the scary little girls who laughed at my home-knitted cardigan but, once summer came and we were all in our blue and white-checked uniforms and the woolly stigma was packed away in the cupboard, we became best friends.

According to our friendship fable, and maybe our mothers, we met for the first time when I was in the bassinet and she was in her pram. Being three months older than me, Helen was smiling and blowing raspberries while I was still gazing blurrily around in amazement, or perhaps it was terror. Our mothers both had a pigeon pair. Helen's big brother Ken would have been keen to play with my big brother but Paul would almost certainly have clung to my mother's swirly skirt and refused to budge. Helen and I wouldn't have even noticed each other that day but ours was the friendship that has stuck, with its ups and downs, for over sixty years.

Helen says her earliest memory of me is when we were three and we were at the tennis with our mothers who were having a hit-and-giggle in their short white dresses that flipped up as they lunged for the ball. Helen was swinging and sliding in the park with the other kids and I was sitting in my pram outside the small clubhouse, not allowed to get out. Paul sat on a seat near me swinging his legs. It was a well-known fact that my mother didn't like her children to get dirty.

My mother didn't like anything to be dirty, or out of place. Dust belonged outside, but she fought a losing battle in Coolamon because our street wasn't sealed for many years and every passing vehicle added another layer to the mantelpiece. It wasn't uncommon, either, for the day to turn dark brown as a dust storm swept through and if you were caught outside, the farmers' topsoil whipped your face and legs. The wind pushed the fine powdery red grit under doors, through the narrow slits where windows met frames and floors met walls, and even into the cupboards. The ornaments in their places on the mantelpiece became true dust-collectors.

The humans in our house didn't collect dust but we had to stay in our places too. We sat in the same position at the table for every meal, on our own red masonite chair that matched the bold red, black and white square lino tiles.

'Come on, Dianne. It's time to set the table.' My mother's nightly refrain.

The red laminex table was set with a tablecloth for every meal; the older, faded, blue checked seersucker for breakfast: the cheerier orange seersucker for lunch, or dinner as it was called then; and the newest, brightest flowery cloth for tea, which I now call dinner. The very best white damask was only for special occasions. The bread and butter plate was placed on the left with the bread and butter knife, then the fork, placemat, and bigger knife. The spoon was placed at the top of the square: a sure sign, I have since been told, that a family lacked class, but my mother learnt to do it like that at her English mother's knee, and she did it the same way as the Queen.

Dad was always served first. He sat at one end of the table, ashtray close at hand, with his back to the two sash windows, his head just missing the thermometer that hung on the wall between them. In the warmer months, these windows were fully open and we ate with the pungent perfume of the yellow broom bush up our noses. Paul sat to Dad's right, and I sat on his left. Mum sat at the other end, close to the stove and cupboards, with her back to the door into the lounge room. When our first shiny television set with the skinny splayed legs was ensconced in the corner of the lounge room, Dad watched the news and weather through the door while he was eating. Paul and I craned our necks trying to see the picture too and Mum sat with all of us staring straight past her, scowling.

Very occasionally she erupted. 'Turn it off. I'm sick of it. Can't we eat in peace?'

Dad wasn't always home to watch the news but he was supposed to be.

'I put my foot down early on,' Mum told me, 'when you and Paul were little kiddies. Your father acted like he was single, not coming home for dinner, not paying attention to any of us. I got sick of cooking his tea and watching it spoil. One night I was so mad I threw it to the chooks. He was cranky when he came in. Where's my dinner? In the chook yard, I told him. He picked you kids up and took you to Mama's. Said he didn't want his children to be around such a bad-tempered woman. Then he came back and we had it out. I told him if he wanted to have his tea on the table, he had to be home by seven o'clock.'

Helen's father stayed out a lot later than Dad but it never seemed to affect the air in their house. When Uncle Les did come home, he was usually in a good mood and whistled while he cleaned Helen's shoes for school the next day. You never knew what mood my father would bring home with him, and Mum was often cranky, so Paul and I trod carefully. If Dad was in a nasty mood, Mum's glacial silence would crack and, in my bed, I would try to block out the raised voices. A few times I heard my mother cry, and when that happened, I burrowed further under the covers sure that life was coming to an end.

I couldn't imagine Helen's father ever making her mother cry. Life always seemed relaxed and mellow at their house, even though Aunty Gwen worked up at Iverach's shop on the haberdashery counter all week and had three children and a house to look after. Like Mum, she didn't drink or smoke but she didn't seem to mind that other people did. She was always warm and welcoming, even to one of the Diannes in their street when she turned up on Helen's birthday saying Helen had invited her to the party. There was no party planned, and there had been no invitation, but Aunty Gwen made one happen so that little girl wouldn't be disappointed.

If it wasn't for Johnny Williamson's house, I would have been able to see Helen's back door from my front door, but we weren't allowed to cut through his yard. Instead, we cut across the church paddock on our corner, scrambling on hands and knees up the steep little slope to get into it. Eventually, to save ourselves the scramble, we fashioned steps, chipping away at the rock-hard earth with a mattock from our shed. We wore a track across the paddock, walking each other home, back and forth, back and forth, loath to say goodnight, until the wee started running down our legs and we'd have to do a quick squat.

Aunty Gwen said I didn't have to knock on their door, I could walk straight in. Helen didn't knock on our front door either. She stood at our front gate and called me, a safe distance from my mother's severity. We didn't play at my house much at all, which suited me, because if I wasn't there I couldn't get into trouble and, besides, I was mortified by the rules and austerity.

'Your place is weird,' Helen would say. 'Your mother's cranky all the time.'

I would hang around Helen's place until she got sick of me and told me to go home, or until Mum sent Dad or Paul to fetch me.

Dad didn't knock either. He just stood out the front and bellowed. 'Dianne! Dianne! Come on, it's time to go. Come out here now.'

My body would droop and I'd drag myself home.

I wanted to be like Helen so much but not because of the dolls that spilled over her bed and along a shelf. I had a doll. What I wanted was a little brother like she had, as well as a smart and handsome big brother, and I wanted to learn to play the piano like she did. Mama even had a piano that I could practise on.'

'Please, Mum,' I begged from the darkness of my bedroom, 'please can I?'

I never was allowed to learn the piano and every Wednesday afternoon I envied Helen when she strolled half a block to have her knuckles rapped by Gwen Confoy, the unmarried sister of the unmarried identical Confoy twins who owned the barbershop. Helen learnt to play so well that she played the piano for Sunday school and at the Sunday school concert, and I continued to tap out 'After the Ball is Over' with one finger on Mama's piano.

At Christmas time, Helen was allowed to open her presents as soon as she woke up but there was no eager tumbling from our beds to the Christmas tree. We had to wait: until after church, after Dad got up, after Mama and Pa arrived, after everyone had a drink and some snacks and were settled in the lounge room. Then and only then could we hand out the presents under our tree. By that time, the presents themselves were almost bursting open with anticipation, especially the ones I'd so carefully made and wrapped.

'Oh, look at that. Thank you, Dianne. This paper-plate letter holder with the ric-racking will be so handy.'

'Yes, I always wanted a bowling cloth with my initials embroidered on it. How did you know?'

Helen was allowed to rip the paper off in a frenzy and crumple it into a ball. Every wrapping in our house had to be worked loose at the sticky tape and folded neatly ready for the next year, and the year after that. Mum was still using the same wrapping paper forty years later, and the same Christmas decorations.

We always had Christmas dinner up at Mama and Pa's and once again I almost died from waiting: for the men to come home from the back bar at the pub, for the turkey and baked vegetables to be ready, for the kitchen to be entirely free of any incriminating evidence of the feast we had just enjoyed, and finally, for everyone to refresh their drinks and to settle into a position with an ashtray handy. By the time we handed out the presents under Mama's silver-painted tree skeleton, and Pa gave Paul and me our shared present, a moneybox full of threepences and sixpences that he had saved all year, sometimes amounting to two pounds each, Helen was playing her new games with cousins and friends.

My presents, for birthdays and Christmas, usually included any necessary items like socks, underpants and hankies. There might be a book, *Girls' Stories*, or something like that, and occasionally something frivolous. The year Paul was given a cowboy and Indian tent, my parents gave me my one and only doll. She wore a wedding dress, and Mama had made her a small collection of other clothes too. She had black hair just like my mother's, and twinkling blue eyes. She was made of a soft rubber, soft enough that Johnny Williamson's little sister was able to bite three of the fingers off. My doll never had a name because I couldn't make the commitment: I changed it every time I played with her. Sometimes she was Fay, after Gail and Wendy Inch's mother, who also had black hair and was very sad because her husband had died. Sometimes she was Gillian, because I thought I would like to have been called that.

Helen and I baptised our dolls secretly in the font at the Presbyterian church. The doors were never locked in those days, so we could sneak in and play in its quiet, sunlit space, peeking behind the organ and under the pulpit, pretending to be the minister, enjoying the feel of being on the stage instead of in the audience. It was much more fun than the Sundays, when the minister droned on and old people listened with their eyes closed, their heads dropping occasionally to their chests. Helen and I, and Jan, our fellow Presbyterian, would nudge each other and dissolve into giggles.

'Shhh!' my mother would chide us. 'Shhh!' she'd whisper again. 'Take a deep breath, Dianne. Stop that. I'm warning you.'

When Jan, Helen and I were chosen to read together from the Bible, we stood facing the congregation in our well-ironed dresses, our hats anchored with elastic under our chins, and snorted, giggled and hiccupped our way through the text, until the minister sent us back to our seats and my mother tutted menacingly.

We played in the Sunday school hall more often than in the church. On its ancient crusted stove, we would try to invent new recipes with ingredients pilfered from our mothers' kitchens. When the minister appeared at the door, we would offer him a cup of tea and a piece of our cake.

One day we decided to be striptease dancers but I was the silly duffer who agreed to go first.

'You go first. Go on. Are you scared?'

'The minute he walked in the joint,' they sang as I danced around the stage. Suddenly they froze: the minister had walked in.

I was down to my singlet and undies and fled red-faced into the little kids' room.

'I think it's time you girls went home,' he said sternly.

I never wanted to go to my home and Aunty Gwen said I was always welcome, so I slept at Helen's place as often as I could.

'I don't know what's wrong with staying home,' my mother would grumble. 'You might as well pack your bags and go and live there.'

'Please, Mum,' I'd whine.

'Oh, I suppose you can, but be back first thing in the morning. I don't know what your father will say.'

I couldn't imagine him saying anything, just humphing. He probably wouldn't even notice I was gone. I never saw him much anyway. He hadn't even been there when I made my first movements into the world: Mama had to drive Mum to the hospital, and look after Paul while she was away, and then it was Mama who had delivered us home from the hospital too. Dad was playing golf. My father had never pushed my pram, changed my nappy, burped or fed me. In fact, there isn't even a photo of him holding me.

Helen only ever stayed one night at our house and we weren't allowed to share my single bed like we could at her place. Instead, we had to open out the hard, scratchy lounge and spent the night rolling into the middle. We didn't dare make a noise either. Mum was too scary. At Helen's place, we whispered and giggled for hours.

'You girls go to sleep,' Uncle Les would shout, banging on the wall. 'Do you hear me? No more talking. Go to sleep, I said. Girls, go to sleep. I won't say it again.'

But he would.

Sometimes, in bed, Helen and I practised being boyfriend and girlfriend, pretending we were on a date, and teaching ourselves how to kiss. We'd seen it at the pictures, and on the front of some books: lips to lips. In the middle of the night after one of our practice sessions, I woke up absolutely busting to go to the toilet. I'd never wanted to go so badly and I'd never ever needed to go in the middle of the night. It really confused me; I didn't know why it was happening. Then my stomach plummeted and I felt ill. Oh my God, I said to myself, I'm pregnant, and Helen's the father!

*

'Play Monopoly,' Helen read from a small square of paper.

'No way, I don't want to do that. I hate Monopoly. Paul always wins. What's the next one?'

We were bored and listless, sprawled across the kitchen table at my house for a change. We'd decided to write everything we could think of on scraps of paper and draw the winner out of a hat.

'We'll do the first one that comes out, okay?' we agreed.

'We could walk out to Lewington's,' I read.

'Nah, it's too far. We could write a play and perform it.'

'Nah, I don't want to do that.'

We picked every piece of paper from the hat, rejecting each idea in turn, until the hat was empty. We hadn't found anything to do but we'd filled in some time at least.

Time passed at the pace of a funeral cortège in Coolamon. Every day blended into the next with little to interrupt the monotony reflected in the sweeping paddocks surrounding the town: fallow and brown during the sowing season, a sea of green if there was rain, shimmering gold in the heat, littered with hay stooks and stalk stubs after harvesting. New haystacks built like houses with pitched roofs would break up some of the tedium of the roads stretching out of town in almost straight lines: to Ganmain, nine miles west, Marrar, nine miles east, Wagga to the south-east, and Ardlethan and Ariah Park to the northwest.

Luckily for Helen and me, Coolamon had raised the money to build a town pool the year we were born. I can't imagine what people used to do before that to escape the throbbing summer heat. Not only did I get to cool off a few blocks from home but Helen and I were never bored diving for stones, learning to do somersaults, or jumping on the trampoline. Sometimes we dived in and kissed under water; other times, we competed to see who could stay kneeling on the bottom the longest while reciting the Lord's Prayer.

It was sixpence to get through the gate, and I'd have sixpence to spend on a paddle pop or a packet of chips. Some days when we stepped outside intending to go home, chilly from the cool air and shade, the heat would sledgehammer us back through the gates.

'Please, can we come in again? We don't want to go home just yet.'

'All right, come on. But make up your mind before you go next time will you, or you'll have to pay another sixpence.'

A wire fence separated the pool from the bowling club where my father spent his weekend days. As we swam and larked in the water, we would hear the occasional riff of laughter, or an exclamation of disgust as the balls clocked into each other and ended up in the gutter. There was a gate in the fence and on hot summer nights after another sun-bleached day Mum would pack a picnic tea and Dad would walk through to join us under the trees beside the water.

When the pool season ended, Helen and I wandered aimlessly around the lanes and streets down our end of town, dragging sticks through the dust discussing the colour of our wedding dresses, who we'd choose for bridesmaids (I was going to have five), how we'd live next door to each other and how our children would marry each other. One of our favourite haunts was the cemetery, where we squeezed out tears at the babies' graves, laughed at funny names, visited our relatives, and soberly assessed the fresh flowers on the mounds of the latest young lad to die from going too fast in his car.

'When we grow up, we'll be the caretakers here,' we agreed, surveying the sadness of the dry, stony ground where even the weeds struggled bedraggled. 'We'll tidy it all up, we'll weed it, plant flowers around the graves, and have some green lawn between the rows. That'll make it much nicer.'

Until that time came, we had to look for inspiration elsewhere. Occasionally, we raided Uncle Les's cigarette butts that he stored in a jar in a cupboard on their back veranda. We practised our smoking in a deserted bulk bin nearby, always hoping that nobody would decide to store their wheat there at that exact moment, or we'd hang out Helen's bedroom window when her parents were at work. When her little brother surprised us, we threw our butts into the grass and slammed the window shut, crossing our fingers that we wouldn't start a fire.

We even offered to clean up Thelma Smith's sewing room. Thelly lived alone in a small cottage at the bottom of my street. She had a big room with a large table in the middle piled high with fabrics. Crumpled heaps of material were flung on every surface around the walls and in the corners. Helen and I were sure there must be buried treasure underneath it all and we sidled around the room, running our fingers over the shiny and velvety fabrics, and lingering over someone's half-made sparkly ball gown.

'Who's this for, Thelly?'

'Oh, this is so gorgeous. Whose is this?'

'Oh, you girls,' she'd puff, waddling her bulk around the room, pins stuck in her mouth, tape measure around her neck.

'Can we help, Thel? Can we tidy up this pile for you? We'd really like to do it. We can fold, can't we, Dianne?'

'We're very good at folding. Can we, please?'

'Shoo', she'd say gruffly. 'You girls get on home. Go on. I don't need any tidying up. Go and play somewhere else.'

Thelly did all the sewing when your own mother couldn't. She made my blue velvet dress for Aunty Marg's wedding, stuffing it into a bag when Mum sent me down to pick it up.

'Goodness me,' Mum humphed. 'Has she got a problem with folding things nicely? Look at this! Oh, that woman!'

Every morning, without fail, Thelly rolled her lopsided body up the street to the shops, collecting bread and paper orders from Mrs Abbey and Mrs Iverach on the way. She lived to be a hundred, still in her house, and, I imagine, still surrounded by scraps of material from our mothers and grandmothers.

We were sure there was treasure, too, in Mrs Vandewater's jam-packed little cottage at the top end of our street. Nothing in there had seen the light of day for decades, but our curiosity was dashed again. She didn't want our help either.

There was nothing for it but to appoint ourselves the caretakers of the Sunday school. Nobody could have a problem with that surely? Judging by the cobwebs and the windows that you couldn't see out, the hall hadn't had more than a cursory lick and polish for about a decade. We would fix that.

Every Saturday for a couple of years, we scrubbed and dusted, put fresh flowers in vases and stuck up pictures of Jesus with all the little children, the Good Samaritan, the Prodigal Son, and Joseph's coat of many colours. We basked in the Sunday morning praise.

'Oh, look at this. How wonderful. Thank you, girls. It looks beautiful.'

Once the inside space had been brought under control, we set about making a garden down the side of the church with a proper path leading into the hall. We planted geranium cuttings along the brick fence to act as a backdrop to our grand vision of 'Sunday school' spelt out in alyssum. Unfortunately, there was no dirt, just stones on top of rock. The geraniums struggled but we watered them diligently and urged them on.

'My mother thinks you're stupid,' the minister's little son told us one day.

His grubby face was watching us from his perch on top of the fence. He wasn't wearing any underpants and we could see everything. Snot was pooling on his top lip and Helen and I looked at each other in disgust.

'Just go away, for God's sake,' one of us muttered.

'My father says people shouldn't swear. My father says that saying God! is swearing. My father says people who swear won't go to heaven.'

'Go away,' we said again, pulling up dead geraniums dejectedly.

'My mother says you'll never grow anything here and you might as well stop trying,' his whining voice went on. 'She says it's a waste of time. She says…'

'Here,' I said, sweetly. 'Take these geranium roots home to your mother and ask her to cook them for you.'

'Yes,' joined in Helen. 'Tell her to grill them. They're delicious like that. And the blacker the root, the tastier they are.'

'Gee, thanks,' he said, running off.

'And make sure you put tomato sauce on them,' I called out after him.

He was back pretty smartly, while we were still laughing. His face was thunderous. 'My mother says you're being rude to me. She doesn't like you. I don't like you.'

'We don't like you much either, so we're even.'

Thankfully, that minister was moved to another parish soon afterwards and the frost in church on Sundays lifted. A new minister arrived and he was so impressed by our industriousness in the hall and the garden that, even though we were only twelve, he asked us to be Sunday school teachers. We graciously agreed.

6

'Mum? What's a prostitute?' Paul asked one night in the kitchen.

We were waiting for Dad to come home so we could have tea, licking at teaspoons of Vegemite to stave off the hunger pangs. I heard Mum's sharp intake of breath and saw her lips press tightly together. The saucepan lids on the stovetop clattered as she checked on the vegetables.

'What do you want to know that for? Where did you hear about that?'

'Dunno. Just heard it somewhere.'

'Well, don't talk about it and don't say that word again. We don't talk about it in this house.'

'But what is it?'

Her face reddened. 'Well, if you must know,' she said, slamming the lid back on one of the triangular saucepans, 'it's a nasty woman who steals other women's husbands. Now stop asking such silly questions and check the fire hasn't gone out. Dianne, you finish setting the table. Come on.'

Fancy stealing someone's husband! I thought. Would someone try to steal Dad?

My father never seemed interested in women at all: not the pretty women on television or the page-three models in the *Daily Telegraph*. Not even Mum. He gave her the requisite peck on the cheek when he was coming or going, but I never saw them kiss on the lips or cuddle just for the heck of it.

'He used to call me Darling,' Mum told me, 'and then he shortened it to Darl.'

I only ever heard him call her Dull.

'Your father didn't like touching me,' she told me decades later during one of our forensic analyses of their marriage, a not uncommon discussion after Dad died.

'If we were travelling on a bus together and our arms touched,' she continued grumpily, 'he'd jerk away as if he'd been electrocuted. It was like sitting next to a plank.'

I was surprised because I thought that would have suited my mother down to the ground, not being touched. She never seemed to like anything to do with sex; she thought it was dirty and disgusting. She tried to teach me that with the strap the day she saw Johnny and me through the sleepout window. She tried too, another time, after Paul was moved into his sleepout bedroom.

We had shared a room until the day we were standing on our beds batting balloons at each other and he stretched to catch one and the back of his pyjama pants ripped. We thought it was hilarious and he showed me his bottom cheek through the tear. Within hours, my eight-year-old brother had been whisked to the front end of the sleepout and my room gradually turned pink: from the flower sprays on the lino, to the bold tuberose floor mat and chenille bedspread, to the embroidered pink posies on the sheer white curtains my mother had made.

I missed Paul when he went, so I scampered into his bed in the mornings.

One day, he told me how the boys at school had been laughing about touching a girl's bottom with their thing. 'Do you want to try and see what it's like?'

'Yes,' I said, thrilled to be let into the bigger kids' games.

We giggled as we tried to manoeuvre ourselves into a position where our bottoms could touch. The next minute, my mother exploded through the door and the air was sucked out of the room. The strap dangled in her hand.

'What are you doing?' she screeched. 'You disgusting children. Dianne, get out of here. Get out of that bed this minute.'

I was paralysed.

She pulled me off the bed, hitting at my legs and bottom with the strap as she shoved me though the door. 'Get to your room and stay there. Dirty girl. I never want to see you in this room again. Don't ever come in here again. Do you hear me?'

Then she turned her attention to Paul. 'And you,' she spat, 'you're a disgrace. You come here. I'll show you what for.'

In my room, I lay on the bed shaking with sobs, blocking my ears so I couldn't hear her angry shouts and the sound of the belt flaying his skin.

I can understand why my mother might have been displeased but I don't understand why she reacted so violently. It wasn't as if she had grown up in a sexless family. She was, after all, one of ten children.

But maybe it was because there had been ten children.

Even the word sex was taboo in our house. Everybody's blood rushed to their faces if it was spoken, and, because it was the sixties, there were a lot of red faces. 'Sexy' was the word of the decade. My mother's face hardened in disapproval whenever it was said on TV, and I cringed. If there was kissing, I became very interested in reading the spines of the books on the bookshelf, sometimes even asking my mother an innocuous question to distract her attention. My insides squirmed when unmarried couples on telly started putting their tongues in each other's mouths instead of dry-lip kissing. They squirmed too when I read one of Dad's paperback Westerns that lived out of sight around the corner of the mantelpiece. I never saw him actually reading any, but those stories were how I learned, surreptitiously, about the benefits of ruby-red lips and the penchant women apparently had for men who were tough, a bit rough, and monosyllabic. I'm surprised my mother let them stay on the mantelpiece. Compared to those, the rest of the reading in our house was very demure: *Reader's Digests*, a couple of old *Boy's Own* books of Dad's, Nino Carlotta's *They're a Weird Mob*, a Shirley Temple picture book, a picture book about the Queen when she was a princess, and a tatty, hardback novel of Mum's called *Eva Layton* that is still on my bookshelf today. The most interesting and out of place book in the house was a slim leather-bound, illustrated copy of *The Rubaiyat of Omar Khayyam* – 'To Ross from Mother, Xmas 1948'.

Sex wasn't the only taboo word in our house of course. We couldn't say poo or wee, for example: it had to be Number One or Number Two. I was, however, allowed to say pregnant, which I wasn't allowed to say when I was at Helen's house.

'Don't say that,' Aunty Gwen gasped when I told her Aunty Gene was pregnant. 'It's not nice. Just say she's expecting. Dear, oh dear,' she tutted, shaking her head.

I never knew what might set my mother off. I knew not to mention or ask about anything that was connected with boys and girls together, or with having babies. I couldn't even ask her if it was true that you could get pregnant if you held hands with a boy, as someone had told me, or if you kissed, as many of us believed. That's what seemed to happen in the pictures: a man and woman kissed and the next thing you knew they had a baby.

Then came the day Harold Holt was lost at Portsea and I, along with the rest of the population, was riveted in front of the television watching the search unfold. I was sitting on our ungiving lounge in my favourite orange, white and yellow striped cotton shift when I became aware that my undies felt wet, as if I had weed myself a bit. I bent over and looked up my shift and a gong clanged in my head. I felt giddy with trepidation. There was a dark spot on my pants. I'd been at Deirdre's house and at Valda's house when the same thing had happened to them. Now it was my turn.

I sidled nonchalantly past my brother and mother, my heart beating wildly, and headed to the toilet. Yes, it was blood.

I knew I had to tell my mother, but I was terrified. I was going to be crossing a paddock full of landmines. One misstep, one mis-word, would cause her to explode. My pulse throbbed loudly in my ears as I crept back inside and stood next to her chair, picking at the black flecks in the upholstery. I took a deep breath, counted to three, then chickened out and started counting again. I didn't know what to say.

Finally, in a whisper, I just blurted it out. 'Mum, I've got blood on my pants.' Immediately, I felt sick with dread. A few days before, when I'd been washing up, I'd come over all hot and dizzy.

'One day soon you might find a spot on your pants,' my mother had said.

But she didn't say what the spot would be: I wasn't supposed to know it was blood. Now my mother would know that I knew, that I had been talking about it with other girls and she would go into a rage.

'Come with me,' she said, and I followed her on shaky legs into my bedroom.

I stood in the middle of the room with the light cord dangling next to my face.

'Wait here,' she said as she left the room.

My stomach twisted, sure that she was going to come back with the strap, but instead she came back with a little booklet in her hand.

'Here,' she said, 'read this. This will explain it all to you.'

Relief washed through me. Is this all that was going to happen? She was just going to give me a book? On the cover there was a pretty blonde teenage girl in a shimmering white dress leaning wistfully against a flowery pole. I'd been waiting a couple of years to look like that girl. I'd seen her before but I couldn't tell my mother that. Whenever she went out to one of her CWA, PWA or P&C meetings, I'd roam through the house hoping to find something that showed that my family was more interesting than it seemed. In Dad's cupboard, I poked about in the black leather case that carried his Masonic gear. Nobody but a Mason was ever supposed to open these cases but Dad's was never locked. I fingered the blue and white satin sash and the leathery apron with its strange compass-like insignia, and leafed through the pages of the little black book that seemed to be just like a Bible. My mother's drawers had proved more interesting. Underneath her velvety church gloves, I'd found this booklet. I knew that it must have something to do with me and that one day it would be mine. So, what with it, and the girls at school, I was better prepared for my spot of blood than my mother.

'Just wait here,' she said to me again. 'I haven't got what you need, so I'll just pop next door. Beverley's home and she might be able to help.'

I was mortified. Now everybody would know.

Many years later, I found out that my mother had been mortified about her periods too and she'd had to use torn-up old sheets for pads.

'When I started working at Black Mountain CSIRO in Canberra,' she told me, 'I had to keep the used rags in my bag and take them home to wash out at night. I was so conscious of the smell and worried the others would notice that, one day, I tried to put one down the toilet. It blocked up, of course, and I felt so embarrassed and ashamed. One of the girls told me about the new sanitary pads you could buy so, when I got my first pay, I bought some. Mother found them and confiscated them. "Think you're so smart now you're earning your own money, do you?" Grandmother Whitby said. "Well, what's good enough for me is good enough for you. In future, you bring your pay packet home unopened and give it to me. I'll decide what you do with it."'

Things hadn't been quite so bad for me after all: my mother let me have pads, but she didn't let me wash my hair when I was bleeding.

'It's not good for you,' she explained curtly, 'and you might catch a chill.'

I felt dirty enough anyway. My mother's disgust about anything to do with 'down there' had seeped into my soul. Now my shame was augmented monthly by an uncomfortable surfboard between my legs which never stayed in the right place, so my pants and sheets were always bloody; a face full of pimples; a bloated belly; and greasy lank hair. Everybody in town knew when I had my periods because of how I looked, but also because of the suspiciously shaped brown paper bag I had to carry home from the chemist, and, in summer, because I couldn't go swimming.

When we went to Culburra the summer after Harold Holt disappeared, I really wanted to swim at the beach.

'Can I use a tampon, Mum?' I asked under cover of darkness.

'I don't know, Dianne. Only married women should use those.'
'Some of the girls in my class use them. Can I please?'
'Oh, all right.'

As I undid the packet of tampons, which came with their own little inserter tubes, my body shivered with excitement. My life was about to change. I would be sophisticated, like the girls in the ads who wore white bikinis. I went into the toilet full of hope but that was soon dashed. I didn't know where to put it. I didn't know there was a specific hole, or if I did, I couldn't find it. I pushed and I shoved and I manoeuvred that little tube, at times weeping with frustration, until finally, my body rebelled: cramps clenched my insides and forced me into a foetal position for what was left of the day. The vomit bucket stayed close. The next day, I accepted my fate and threw the box of tampons into the bottom of my suitcase.

'I can't use tampons,' I told my friends back in Coolamon. 'They make me sick.'

The same cramping misery very soon became part and parcel of my bloody monthly routine. Their intensity increased and sometimes Mum would have to pick me up from school. My rosy cheeks would go a greenish shade of pale, the voices of my friends and the playground sounds came to me through thick layers of cotton wool, and everything looked like it was on a snowy black and white television. The doctors said 'more salt'. They said 'less salt'. Eventually they just said 'valium'. Now I really was growing up: I even had my own pills.

*

The last time my mother left bruises on me, I was fourteen, in second form. I still cowered and cringed when the strap came out but at some point, probably during one of the laundry lashings, I'd made the subconscious decision to never cry in front of my mother again. I saved my tears for under the blankets at night when my body could convulse unashamedly.

The blankets started providing cover for my most fervent prayers as well, and it was Johnny's cousin, Chris, who sparked that off. Chris was a couple of years older than me and had been off school sick for a long time. He was now just in the year above me. At assembly one Monday morning, I caught him looking at me. He smiled but I was startled and too timid to smile back.

I still felt like the same dumpy girl with the bad hairdo and knee-length dress in the front row of our first form school photo, the daggy one whose bra was made by her mother. I may have loved its well-fitted soft cotton against my skin and it may have had little blue and pink flowers before patterned bras were even available in the shops, but I just wanted a bra like all the other girls, a bought one with elastic straps.

'Hey, look at Dianne Lucas's bra,' those girls snorted as we changed in the open-roofed dressing shed at the pool. 'Did your Mummy make that for you? Go on. Show us. Ha, your mother's such a weirdo. Fancy making a bra, and it hasn't even got elastic straps. You're such a dag, Lucas.'

Chris started seeking me out at lunchtime, casually sitting next to me on the bench against the Home Science room. 'Hi,' he'd say.

'Mmm, hi,' I'd stutter, scarcely able to breathe, hoping nobody would notice. It would be something else for the girls to tease me about.

'How's things?' he'd ask.

'Um, good.'

His hands would rest on the edge of the wooden bench as he joked with some of the kids playing near us. My gaze would settle on those hands, liking to see them more each day. I wondered what it might be like to touch them. I was aware of his firm body rippling the air next to me. Before, when he played football, he had a quick, sturdy body and I remembered his muscly legs in the footy shorts. Now, unlike the other boys, he usually wore long pants and they made him seem quite grown-up.

'I'm embarrassed about my legs,' he told me one day. 'They're so pale and skinny since I've been sick.'

'Will you play again?' I asked.

'Nah, I don't think so.'

Chris was the first boy to make my stomach flip. I'd been in class with the same boys since kindergarten and went to church and Sunday school with most of them too. I'd known the new kids who joined us in first form from the local St Michael's Primary School most of my life too. There had been only one tubby, red-cheeked boy who I didn't know and, when he took a liking to me, I didn't want to know him.

'Hey, Tippo,' the boys would chortle. 'Do you want to kiss her? Pucker up, Dianne.'

He seemed to enjoy it, but I just felt sick and embarrassed, mortified to have that sort of attention. Not as mortified as I would become, though, when Paul told me what Johnny had said.

'Ha ha!' he whooped at me one day. 'Willo said he wouldn't mind getting into your pants. Ha ha ha!'

I felt like I'd been kicked in the stomach. I was afraid something was leaking out of me, a miasma that smelt of body and sex. I prayed my mother never found out and I didn't look at Johnny again for years. I hid in my room whenever he was around. Every pore on my skin zinged with vigilance.

Now I was aware in a different kind of way and, even though Chris's eyes crinkled with smiles when he saw me, I never dared believe that he actually liked me. He's probably just being nice, I told myself, or feels sorry for me.

Every day, I expected to never see his smile again, and every night, under the covers, I prayed, offering my soul to God, if only Chris would look at me and smile the next day. 'Please, please, please, just let him look at me. Let him like me. Please God, please. I'll do anything. I'll be good for Mum. I'll be a nicer person. Just please, God, please.'

And the next morning, as we turned to march to our respective classrooms, my prayers would be answered and he'd smile and sometimes wink. My muscles would melt and I'd thank God.

Maybe that's why I kept being a Sunday school teacher. Maybe God did exist and I wasn't just minding the little kids until church was over.

Chris was the second eldest of eighteen kids and my pulse raced when I saw any of them. I craved to have something that was his, to feel like part of his life, so I tried to remember all his brothers and sisters' names, reciting them as I went to sleep at night, but the smallest ones, and their birth order, often eluded me. Instead, I memorised their car's number plate.

With my mother's strict control of my movements, Chris and I really only saw each other at school, or from afar at the footy, but sometime during that year a few of the older kids in town started a youth club. One of its first activities was a dance, held, much to my parents' disgust, in the CWA rooms.

'Why did they agree to that?' snarled Dad. 'It's a ridiculous idea.'

'I don't know,' sighed Mum. 'They thought it would be the safest way, and we can keep an eye on it.'

'Can I go? Can I go?' I bounced.

I was eventually allowed to go, but only with a strict curfew and on condition that Dad dropped me off and picked me up.

I danced with Chris – the first time I had touched him. We barely shuffled to the slow tunes, our arms around each other's necks, just like everyone else. Standing out the front of the small CWA hall, on the footpath of the town's main street where we had gone for a breath of fresh air, Chris kissed me, twice: once on the forehead, and once on the cheek. Every cell in my body cheered: he likes me. I couldn't believe how soft his lips were, and I wanted to feel them again, but we needed to be back inside before my father came. It was to be the only time I ever felt his lips on my face. He kissed my hand once too, the only time we ever held hands.

The youth club had organised a bus trip to Wagga to go ten-pin bowling and to the pictures. My parents insisted I could only go if there was a chaperone, and that, of course, had to be my mother. Was it me she didn't trust? Nobody else's parents worried about a bunch of kids who'd grown up together going out for a fun day in Wagga. Did she know that Chris and I smiled at each other or that he'd taken advantage of my cheek and forehead?

If it wasn't mortifying enough that my mother came, I had to wear my best dress, the lemon eyelet-voile one with the cinched waist and wide belt that she'd made me for special occasions, like going to Wagga. It may have only been twenty-five miles away but, for our family, it was still quite an expedition that was only made once or twice a year – and we always had to dress up for it. Everyone else wore jeans. My pretty dress ended up with a grubby black front courtesy of the bowling balls, and my stockings snagged and sagged.

I didn't want to sit with my mother when we went to the pictures, I wanted to sit with Chris, and so I manoeuvred myself into the middle of the pack with him, where she couldn't reach me. That didn't stop her, though, and after some humiliatingly fierce whispering, Marianne Smith was sat between us, a couple of rows behind my mother. Chris and I held hands behind Marianne's back for the whole film.

I wasn't allowed to attend any other youth club activities after that and it didn't last much longer anyway. I wouldn't have been surprised if my parents didn't have a major hand in its demise, the only extracurricular activity that had ever been available to me. There were always Cubs and Scouts for the boys, at least.

I blame Helene Davis, Mum's friend, for what happened next. She was the first person I knew who wore mirrored sunglasses, so you could never tell where she was looking. She'd take up a position at the pool where she could see what everyone was doing and scan for gossip to share with the mothers.

Summer was tailing off and I was feeling more at ease with Chris, able to hold my own in a conversation and more confident under his tender gaze. One gloriously sun-loving day at the pool, we were lying next to each other on our towels on the grass at the edge of the concrete at the deep end of the pool – the big end, we called it. Our chins were cupped in our hands and we were chatting idly as we watched the shenanigans in the water a couple of yards away.

'Watch your sister on the high board. She's a good diver. I always hurt my head when I hit the water.'

'You're a good swimmer, though,' he said.

Suddenly, my mother appeared at the pool entrance. She swung her eyes around and they alighted on us at the far end. My insides quailed, because I knew why she was there. She hadn't come to tell me the dog had died or to ask what I wanted for dinner, but to catch me out, to humiliate me publicly. I decided to be brave. We weren't doing anything wrong: our towels were hardly touching. She marched straight for us, her face grim, her mouth set in disgust mode. Heat from her disapproval washed over me as she came near. I hadn't moved, transfixed by the coming storm. I was aware of every atom of air on my body but the screeches, splashes and laughs from the water were muffled.

She loomed over us, ignoring Chris, and hissing at me. 'Get up, get your things and get out of here. You're coming home with me, young lady. Now.'

She hauled me up by my ear as I scrabbled for my clothes and towel. She marched me out of the pool, ear first, past the boy's dressing shed, past the kids sucking on ice blocks, the kids lying on the hot cement warming up after their swim, and past the kids craning over the lolly counter at the kiosk. She pushed me through the turnstile and out the front door.

There was a car waiting for us: to my shame, Aunty Mavis, Pa's cousin and a close friend of the Lucas women, was the chauffeur. Aunty Mavis had no children, played golf, enjoyed a tipple, and crocheted all her clothes except her underwear. She had a nose for looking down and was never short of a sniff and critical commentary about everyone else's business.

Nobody spoke during the few blocks to home but my head was filled with noise.

'Thank you, Mavis. I don't know what I'd do without you,' I heard Mum say as I walked stiffly into the house.

I was fuming at the injustice, devastated by the indignity, and terrified of what was to come, but I didn't slam any doors. I didn't want to do anything to upset my mother any further. I headed straight to my bedroom, hoping that she'd had enough, but she hadn't.

She came in with the strap as I was trying to get damp togs down my shaking legs with trembling hands. I ignored her and tried to appear calm. I thought that if I stayed calm she might listen to me for a change and see that I hadn't done anything wrong, but her rage filled the room. I backed into my clothes cupboard and cowered as she struck. The cupboard wobbled and knocked against the wall. Once again, there was no escape, and once again my skin would bear the red, blue and purple marks of her disgust.

'How dare you! How dare you lie there like that with him? You're turning into a right little tart. You disgust me. Who do you think you are, young lady? I know where you'll end up. I've seen him. Oh yes, I've seen what he does. I've seen him put his hands down Catherine Livermore's pants. You keep away from him. Do you hear me? DO YOU HEAR ME?'

'Yes, Mum,' I whimpered.

She eased back, victorious once again. 'Now, hang those wet things out and get on with your homework.'

I don't know if it was true about Catherine but she wasn't me: I was the peck-on-the-cheek girl, but you never knew where that might lead, I suppose. I have no memory of seeing Chris after that day, at the pool or at school, but perhaps I just don't want to remember the shame I felt.

7

I tried to keep my head down at home after my so-public humiliation, but it kept bobbing up again. Now it was my father who took the lead in making sure I was on the straight and narrow, the responsibility handed to him by my mother, who felt increasingly resentful and inadequate as my schooling years surpassed hers.

'You're just like your father,' she'd spit at me. 'Too smart for your own good.'

'Ooh, I'm so stupid,' she'd growl when something went awry in the kitchen.

Dad took to his new role with enthusiasm and I never knew when he might strike.

One night, he came home the worse for wear and was holding himself upright in his chair at the kitchen table, looking through to the television with drunken eyes while Paul and I tried to keep out of his line of sight. I needed a form signed to say I could go swimming the next day. I held it out to my mother.

'Get your father to do it,' she muttered.

'Dad, can you sign this for me, please?' I asked, dropping it on the table next to him and scampering back to the lounge room.

Behind me I heard his fist hit the table and cutlery clatter against china. 'Dianne,' he roared, 'get back in here. What's this rubbish? What are you playing at here?'

I slunk into the kitchen, mystified. What had I done?

'What's this?' he demanded, waving the piece of paper in my face. 'What sort of writing do you call this? That's not what you get taught at school, is it?'

'No, Dad.'

In class that day, I'd decided that I didn't like my handwriting. The scrawny forward-sloping letters that had been meticulously drilled into us with pencils and slope-cards, inkwells and blotters, and finally, biros, never changed. My pages always looked like a little kid had written them. I wanted to express myself in a new way, and during a doodling session I discovered an attractive, rounder, backward-sloping style. I'd used it on the note.

'You write properly, young lady. No more of this rubbish,' Dad ranted, drunken spittle gathering at the corners of his mouth. 'You're getting a bit too big for your boots. What did the teachers say about this? Hey?'

On and on he went.

Some weeks later, I borrowed *Mila 18* by Leon Uris from the school library. It was one of the books kept in the glass-door cabinet that stood adjacent to the teacher's desk, the special books for the senior students in that year's trial at having a fifth and sixth form. I'd exhausted all the other books that lined the walls of the library, and there wasn't a public library in the town. The closest thing to it, the School of Arts that nestled into the side of the top pub, had long ago been boarded up and its front yard left to collect the rubbish that swirled about in the winds. The library teacher, recognising my thirst, had let me borrow from the older kids' cabinet.

The book was heavy going, about war, and after the first couple of chapters I dropped it on the floor beside my bed intending to return it unread. The next morning, I rushed out the door and forgot it.

It was, presumably, my mother who found the book, because Dad hardly set foot in my room since the days when he tucked me in and I'd pretend to be a tiger hiding under the sheets and he could never find me.

Having still never read it all these years later, I don't know what brought my father to the veranda outside the headmaster's office, but there he was, gesticulating angrily as the headmaster nodded in reply. I assume there must be some sex in it and that my mother inadvertently opened it to that page when she went in to hoover my floor. If that's what it was, I could imagine the steam coming out of her ears as she slammed the book down in front of Dad as he finished his morning cup of International Roast, black, two sugars.

'Look what rubbish your daughter is reading now,' she'd have said, her face set in disgust.

And that was that: my father insisted that I be banned from borrowing any more books from behind the glass doors, and the teachers were careful not to encourage me outside the strictly set curriculum for my year.

Then Mr Padovan arrived. He was our new third form English teacher. Until then all our high school English teachers had been like the mustard-coloured bloke in first form with the permanent five o'clock shadow who only ever wore clothes in a couple of shades that matched his skin. We slept through his classes. Mr Padovan was very different: he had blond hair that tickled his collar and he rode a motorbike, using a tea towel as a sling when he broke his arm.

The first day when he walked into our classroom, he hung a large black and white poster of a foot over the blackboard. 'Write me a story about the person whose foot this is,' he said.

My pulse beat excitedly. I was so sick of having to write compositions about what I did in the holidays. Was that a speck of light I could see at the end of the Coolamon tunnel?

I went about the tasks Mr Padovan set with my mind whirling. If shoes had springs, if rabbits were as big as people, if you could have someone else's memory, whose would you choose and why? What changes would there be in our daily lives if we gave up the idea of owning things for ourselves? We had to list our fears and I included my father but not my mother.

I wrote essays about misguided university students rioting in the streets, about the futility of protesting South African apartheid in Australia, about how angry I was that the Aboriginal people in Australia and Black people in America were treated so badly, and about how unsafe the streets were. I vented and raged and, in his red-penned loose scrawl, Mr Padovan encouraged me to see things in all their complexity rather than being dogmatic, the first time I'd ever heard the word. When he handed back our work I scanned greedily for his comments.

'Typically effervescent,' he wrote. 'I found your paragraph really funny. Fair dinkum I was in stitches.'

He had me in stitches too.

'I think you must have written this composition while you were having a meal,' he wrote another time. 'You state a number of points and then when you go back to your food you forget about them.'

'I found your hatred for athletics very disheartening', he wrote. 'Surely one who is capable of writing compositions of great length and interest would be able to do at least moderately well at athletics especially the long jump.'

When I submitted a piece of work in which I bemoaned being called Dianne, he told me that the name had great mythological significance and I shouldn't dismiss it so lightly.

I didn't know what he wrote on other people's work but I felt special and like all the other girls, and a few boys, I fell in love with him.

Dad hated him, but he didn't like the Beatles either. 'He's just a long-haired galoot,' he said more than once. 'What's wrong with going to the barber, for goodness sake?'

When it was Mr Padovan's birthday, the only boy in fifth form and I made him a cake. David provided the idea and, because Mum was at a meeting, I provided the kitchen. We blew up a balloon, filled it with water and iced it. We slowly and carefully carried it the few blocks to Mr Padovan's flat and sat it on an outside table, hoping the wobble would settle down before he answered the door.

'Let's cut it out here,' we chorused. 'It's such a lovely afternoon.'

We sang 'Happy Birthday' and 'For He's a Jolly Good Fellow' and he closed his eyes and made his wish.

'Go on. Cut it,' we urged.

The knife descended, and icing and water exploded everywhere. We all shrieked with laughter.

And then my father arrived. Hauling his bulk out of our mushroom-and-white Holden station wagon, there were no hellos or happy birthdays. 'Get in the car, Dianne. Now.'

By the time we got home, Mum was fuming in the kitchen that I'd left in a mess, intending to clean it up before she came home. The walk to Mr Padovan's flat had taken longer than I anticipated.

'When the cat's away the mice will play,' she sneered.

I was afraid she'd reach into the third drawer.

'Sorry, Mum. I was coming back to do it. Really I was.'

'Well, clean it up now, and make a good job of it. And I don't want you hanging around with that Johnston boy again. He's too smart for his own good too, just like you. And don't you dare go to that teacher's flat again. Do you hear me?'

'Yes, Mum,' I responded quietly.

'Now, get busy, or there'll be real trouble.'

Relieved not to have the strap, I worried about what my parents were going to do. Would they bail up Mr Padovan and make a scene? Over the next few days at school, I moved hesitantly, expecting to see some change in the way my favourite teacher treated me, but there was none.

Towards the end of the year, our headmaster decided we should practise our dancing for a school social that was coming up, so on a thickly hot afternoon, the high school classes straggled down to the cavernous Cazna Theatre which used to be a picture theatre, where I first saw *Pollyanna* and fell in love with Hayley Mills. Now it was used for flower shows and school concerts. We stood around in small groups giggling about how weird it was to have to practise dancing.

When the music started, Mr Padovan approached our small group. 'Would you like to dance with me, Dianne? Shall we show them how it's done?'

I could only nod, fully aware of the looks and daggers that were being thrown behind me. I let him steer me around the floor, my face red, my heart beating wildly.

'Do you like to dance?' he asked.

'Um, yes. It's okay. We don't get to do it much. We used to have dancing every Friday morning but that was square dancing.'

I felt proud that he had chosen me first to dance with out of all the other girls. When the song finished, I turned to rejoin the others but he held my arm.

'Had enough, have you?' he laughed. 'Don't you want to dance any more? You haven't had your usual pizzazz lately. Is everything all right? Dancing will help.'

He danced every dance with me that afternoon: I wasn't going to say no. Afterwards, I walked back to school in a confused daze: my heart swollen with happiness from his attention, but its tom-tom beat keeping me aware that the blissful hour I'd just spent made me a target. I felt like I did when I was expecting a storm of rage from my mother, and I didn't have to wait long before I was yanked hard back to earth.

Not all the girls in my class were teasers, but the ones who were could be vicious – in a 1960s Coolamon kind of way, when we had been classmates since kindergarten. My Coolamon skin wasn't very thick and their barbs, often random, hit their target and my shoulders became a bit more hunched over. Besides my homemade bra, they made fun of me because my mother was so proper and my brother was so slow and my father had such a noisy truck, the old Blue Flier. They snorted at me when I knew the answers and whispered behind their hands, snickering at me, when they were bored

'Lubra lips, lubra lips,' they'd sometimes jeer, and every morning I'd put powder on my lips to make them less noticeable.

After I danced with Mr Padovan, they really hated me and as we collected our ports from the school veranda, they jostled me, blocking my way, until one of them couldn't contain herself any longer.

She grabbed my upper arm in a full-skinned horse-pinch that twisted my skin down to the bone. 'Think you're so smart, Lucas. He just feels sorry for you because you're so ugly.'

'Ooh, look, she's gonna cry.'

My arm felt like a burning lump of wood and ached for days. I hid the large plum-sized purple bruise beneath my school cardigan, out of my mother's sight and I buried the delight and confidence that came from having someone pay me attention and liking me far away from the other girls' noses.

Mr Padovan didn't stay longer than that year. I wouldn't be surprised if my father didn't have him run out of town. It wasn't the last I heard of him, though. He knew that I was banned from borrowing out of the senior bookcase in the library, so for the next year he sent me parcels of books on loan, always accompanied by a long letter about the stories and the characters. They were Jane Austens and George Eliots mainly. When I was finished, I would send them back and he would send me another parcel.

Eventually, I let the correspondence drop, too caught up in studying for the School Certificate, and prone to the fickleness of teenage inconstancy. I still regret it. I regret never making the opportunity to ask why. Why me? Why were you so kind to me? What did you see?

8

I spent most of the next couple of years in a state of confusion, and it wasn't only the hormones zinging through my body. Helen and I were in some kind of dance with each other where you swing apart then come back together. Sometimes the swing was far and long but the coming together was usually close and intense.

We started every school year sitting together but rarely finished like that. I was too annoying.

'Stop it, for God's sake,' she'd snap, slapping down my arm when I mindlessly and obsessively twirled the curly ends of my hair. 'It's so bloody irritating.'

And she had a similar reaction to my father when I changed my writing style. 'You can't do that, you dickhead,' she scathed. 'You're not supposed to change how you write. It's inherited. And it looks stupid too.'

Before long, she'd be sitting up the back of our small classroom with the girls who teased me. I'd pretend I didn't care, spending my time with Deirdre and Marianne, who never made fun of me, but before the sun had risen the next day, I'd be pining for her again, wanting my best friend back, something we always called each other even when we weren't speaking. Without her by my side, I felt ill-fitted to the Coolamon world: with her, I could belong. I wasn't all love and adoration, though: as well as being annoying and dependent, I was jealous and envious too.

Helen was the first girl to wear blue and green without a colour in between. She was elected school captain in fourth form and I was runner-up, the girls' prefect who had to stay in Coolamon, at school, while she went to Sydney to meet the Queen and Princess Anne. She was the prettiest of all of us too, with her snub nose and big brown eyes. The boys from Marrar agreed. Every Friday they came in a carload to Coolamon for wool-classing lessons and in their lunch hour they drove up and down the street outside our classroom hoping for a glimpse of Helen, their eyes lighting up when they saw her.

Once a week, I was the luckiest, though: I had her to myself for a double period. While the other kids in our class were learning about commerce or home science, we sat unsupervised in a cupboard-sized room in our demountable classroom doing our fourth form history lesson by correspondence.

On another day, four of us squashed into the same space to do a double period of French by correspondence. French proved just as useful as history, even though Helen wasn't in that class, because I convinced my parents that I needed a record player to play the blue plastic records provided by the correspondence school to help us with our accents. Until then, the family's only music came from a brown bakelite wireless tucked high above the linen cupboard in the kitchen. Other than that, there was only the radiogram up at Mama's where, among her collection of Victor Borge and other obscure piano players, the *Oklahoma* soundtrack and the Pickard Family singing family favourites like 'Roll Out the Barrel', she had records Paul and I listened to when we were young: 'Hiawatha', 'Tubby the Tuba' and 'Ferdinand the Bull'. With my new portable record player, and my first bought single, 'Do It Again' by the Beach Boys, I was ready for the seventies.

'I hope we didn't get this so you could just play this sort of rubbish, Dianne,' warned Mum as I lovingly stroked the small machine that closely resembled a hair dryer.

'No, Mum, I really need it for French. Cross my heart.'

But it was history that I looked forward to every week. Any gripes that had built up between Helen and me fell away and we slipped back into the groove of our childhood, when we'd wandered and talked and plotted and laughed every waking moment. Not much work was done in our cubbyhole and any pretence at fifteen-year-old sophistication flew out the window, or it would have if the windows opened. We giggled and gossiped and did everything but schoolwork. We even started a club: the Purple Pinkie Club. We'd had a club before, again just the two of us, which we called the Peewit Club. Then, we'd stood out the front of each other's houses shrilling 'Peewit' until the other one came running out to play.

The Purple Pinkie Club only ever convened during our history lesson but we had a secret handshake, hooking our pinkies together, that we occasionally used outside the room. We never told anyone else about it, and we had meetings all through our final year at Coolamon Central and even when we started fifth form at Wagga High. Helen was the secretary and social confeener (sic), while I was the president and treasurer. We were both on the committee.

We kept meticulous club records: a social diary, lists of our favourite songs and jokes, and a weekly log of our weight. On the last diet we ever shared, I gained half a stone, and Helen went on a weight-losing spree that resulted in us having to learn a new word for our vocabulary and landed her with the nickname she took to Wagga High – Muscles.

The most diligently kept record in the club was Romances. This was a list of the boys we liked. For a while, they changed every week; sometimes we even had the same one. By the end of the year, though, a name had appeared on my list and maintained its position until long after the club records were abandoned: Billy Marshall.

Billy had been Helen's boyfriend for two weeks during the summer holidays when we were twelve or thirteen. He'd even given her a ring, probably from a sherbet packet. Because she'd already discarded him, I acted blasé in front of her, covering up my increasingly reddening face as he moved from being a silly crush to a full-blown desire. I didn't quite trust that Helen wouldn't use her knowledge against me when she was up the back of the classroom again.

Like Chris, Billy was Johnny's cousin too, and one of the St Michael's Primary School boys who landed in our class in first form. For three years, we had sat in the same classroom and I hadn't taken any notice of him: he was just one of the irritating boys who sat up the back and didn't want to be there. He left school as soon as he turned fifteen. He lived down our end of town so I was used to sharing the footpath up to the main street, to school or the pool, but during that year, the sight of his black curly head floating up the path started making my face flush and my stomach roll. Forty years later, my breath still catches in my chest when I see black curly hair and a confident tall back loping along the street.

By the beginning of the next year, when I was catching the bus at seven thirty in the morning to go to fifth form at Wagga High, I was hungering for glimpses of him. On many mornings, as I walked down to the bus at Logan's garage on the other side of the railway line, Billy would be driven to work in one of the Moseses' snub-nosed red trucks. When I heard the familiar rattle of the truck approaching, my senses would fire up and I'd pray it was him. It was always his hair that I saw first. He'd smile and nod or raise a finger in greeting. Sometimes he craned around to keep watching me. I'd respond with a half-smile and slight hand-lift in acknowledgement: it wouldn't have done to let on that the sight of him sent my blood raging. In stooking season, I'd sometimes see the red truck in one of the paddocks we passed on the way to Wagga, and I'd nonchalantly twist my neck, desperately scanning for a glimpse of him in his white T-shirt and blue jeans. When he'd stop what he was doing and raise his hand, I wanted to believe that wave was just for me.

Around this time, Chris's older brother started a band, Rubber Soul, and they played at dances in St Michael's hall, which was at the back of Mama and Pa's house, and opposite St Michael's, where the nuns used to terrorise the kids and Johnny learnt the trick of jamming his hand up under his armpit to numb it before they gave him the cuts. My father would always drive me there, watching until I was safely inside. I walked the gauntlet of blokes hanging around outside – Billy usually right in the middle of them – with my father's eyes drilling holes in my spine.

'Dianne,' the boys would nod. 'How's it going?'

'Good,' I'd mumble and smile, hoping my father didn't see.

Once inside, I'd stare at the door until his lean body appeared. The first time he asked me to dance, I felt faint. I worried that I'd make a fool of myself by falling over my feet, or his. Even though the lights were low, it was as though we were moving under a spotlight. I could feel the eyes on us – all his non-dancing mates guffawing at his audacity and the sharp dagger looks from the girls who wanted him for themselves.

'Why's he dancing with her?' I could hear them whispering.

It made much more sense that he would be dancing with one of them, a girl whose parents didn't scrutinise her every move, whose parents wouldn't disapprove of her having a boyfriend who was Catholic, had left school early, and was a bit of a lout.

We danced close, our feet barely moving. Beneath his best long-sleeved shirt his body was firm, and I could feel the hard muscles in his arms. I breathed in the sweet aroma of the hair oil that kept his wiry curls glistening. I wanted to remember it in my dreams that night. Before the lights were turned up, and before my father appeared at the door to take me home, Billy kissed me.

It wasn't my first kiss; that had happened when our family was on holiday at Culburra and I'd met a group of boys who were going to Sydney University. Besides introducing me to Jimi Hendrix, one of them had engaged me in a kissing session on the beach. Our teeth clinked together and I thought I might choke. When Billy kissed me, everything fitted together without any bumping or clinking and I could have drunk him down without stopping. When I tasted his lips, every muscle in my body sighed and relaxed and it's a wonder I didn't melt to the floor.

The town footy on Sunday afternoons provided the backdrop for my love affair fantasy. My mother didn't go any more since the day she was standing behind the goalposts talking to a friend and Johnny Kew kicked a goal that whammed into her breast and knocked her over, making her semi-conscious from the pain. Dad always stood with the other men in front of the dressing sheds, where they could analyse the players' moves and give advice as they went on or came off. There was a window of opportunity for me to avoid scrutiny and when I could, I stood with Billy and enjoyed knowing we were sharing the same air.

One day he invited me to sit in his mother's car with him to watch the game. He'd only recently acquired his licence, although not having a licence had never stopped him from whizzing down the road at the wheel of a car. Our breaths made the windscreen fog up and it was hard to see what was happening on the oval, but I didn't care: I was in a cosy, warm bubble and never wanted to leave. When it came time to emerge into the cold wind again, I felt exposed to everybody's judgement. As I walked past people rugged up in their overcoats with red cheeks, I wondered who would be the one to tell my mother, and the rest of them, would they think I was trespassing, that I wanted something I couldn't have, and that I was being silly feeling about Billy the way I did. There were no two ways about it, though: I was in love.

The Grasshoppers, Coolamon's Aussie rules team, were on a winning streak that winter and after the fortnightly at-home games, win or lose, the golf club put on a dance. They let anyone over fifteen go and I was allowed because Dad usually went as well, not to dance, but to prop up the bar. Mum never came; she didn't like going to bars, especially if my father was drinking. Billy and I often ended up together, dancing or covertly holding hands under the table. I was too self-conscious to be comfortable, or to be much of a conversationalist.

'Good game today,' was about the best I could do. 'How come you didn't play?'

'Ah, you know, I missed training.'

'You're always missing training.'

'Yeah, well, I'm so good I don't really need training,' he joked, 'but they won't let you play without it.'

As the siren hooted at the end of the game one Sunday, Billy asked me if I'd go to the dance with him that night.

'What? What did you say?'

'I said do you want to come to the dance with me tonight? I could pick you up. Do you reckon you'll be allowed?'

It was the first time I'd ever been asked on a date. Of course I wanted to go. I wanted to be with him all the time. I wanted to be his girlfriend, to snuggle into his side as he drove so that everyone would know our relationship was serious.

'I don't know if my parents will let me but I'll ask. I'll ring you and let you know. Okay?'

It would be the first time I had spoken Billy's name in our house since the sound of it made the blood rush to my face. I knew it would send the blood to my mother's face but for a different reason: she hadn't liked either of his cousins' names either and I didn't expect her to change now. I never said Billy's name anywhere except in the Purple Pinkie Club meetings, where I pretended he was just a fanciful crush rather than the boy I wanted to marry.

'You're such a dag,' Helen would say if she knew, and being a dag wasn't such a good thing in those days.

When other kids talked about him, I listened greedily feigning disinterest, and straining to keep the flush from my face. I couldn't risk anybody knowing how I felt. I didn't want them to grab his name from me, like they might grab my favourite pen, and tease me with it, holding it just out of my reach. They didn't care about my precious things, and I knew that even if I was with my mother, it wouldn't stop them.

I also knew that just a casual passing the time of day with him outside the butcher shop would set Coolamon tongues awagging and it would find its way back to my mother, in her apron, in our kitchen.

'I saw Dianne up the street, Audry. She was chatting with that Marshall boy.'

With each slash of my mother's strap, I had long ago learnt that feeling warm and happy and liked by a boy meant I was dirty and bad.

'Mum,' I finally said, as she cut the scones for our Sunday night dinner. I'd come into the kitchen a few times with the intent of asking but each time rushing hope had swamped my vocal cords. 'Mum, can

I go to the golf club with Billy Marshall tonight? He asked me and he'll pick me up.'

She clattered the tray into the oven and her face closed down into its grim tightness. 'How will he pick you up?' she scoffed.

'In his mum's car. She said he could.'

'Oh, for goodness sake, Dianne,' she huffed as she stood up, 'what do you want to go with him for?'

'I just do,' I said and then stood silent, waiting.

'I don't know. Why are you always trying to rock the boat? You've just got to push a bit further all the time, don't you?'

'Please, Mum?'

'We'll see about it when your father gets home. Now, haven't you got something you should be doing?'

When Dad came in, he was in a good mood, rubbing his hands together and laughing about something someone had said at the club.

'Your daughter wants to go to the club tonight with Billy Marshall,' Mum announced. 'You decide. I wash my hands of it.'

'Let me think about it,' he said. 'Is dinner ready?'

When he called me back into the kitchen to deliver his verdict, I held my breath.

'All right,' he said, 'you can go, but make sure you're home by eleven o'clock. I'll be there, so I'll be keeping an eye on you, don't you worry.'

The phone was slippery with sweat as I gripped it to call Billy, and my voice shook as I asked his mother if I could speak to him.

'Hello,' came his voice.

'I can come,' I said breathlessly.

'Great,' he laughed. 'I'll pick you up at eight o'clock. Don't be late.'

When he arrived, I walked to our front gate afraid I'd be called back at any moment. I could hear Mum taking her displeasure out on the washing up but when I stepped through the gate, the night air wrapped itself around me.

Billy didn't take me straight to the club. Instead, he took me to his house, where his mother and grandmother sat at the table finishing their cups of tea in their small, warm kitchen. His mother and I had only ever nodded at each other, but I'd known his stepfather all my life. He was a friend of my aunties', Gene and Marg, and, when I was three, he and a mate had dressed up in their clothes for a football do. When they emerged into the dining room from the dark hall all dolled up in dresses with red lipstick and eyeshadow, everyone laughed, except me: I cried. I was confused and scared. I didn't like clowns or Santa Claus either.

'I won't be a minute,' Billy said. 'Just got to change my shirt.'
'Would you like a cuppa?' his grandmother asked me.
'Oh, um, no, thanks. I'm okay. Thank you.'
'Sit down then. You're Ross's girl, aren't you? Live opposite Pat.'
'Yes, that's me.'
'Thought so. That's good. How is your dad?'
'He's good.'

I wanted to stare at everyone and everything. It was strange seeing his mother in her kitchen when I only ever saw her in the car or the main street. She didn't say much but his grandmother chatted on.

'What's your dad's brother's name? Was it Fred?'
'No, Frank. Uncle Frank. He's in Newcastle.'

Billy came back in holding one of his little brothers in a head-lock, ruffling his hair.

'You two going for a dance or what? Are you just going to sit here all night? You can, but the dance might be more fun.'

I wanted to do both.

Billy only ever crossed our threshold once.

'Billy's coming to visit me tonight,' I told my mother as I set the table for dinner. I was getting braver, saying his name, but there was still the wobble in my voice and the heat in my face.

'Is that right?' she sniffed.
'We're going to watch the tennis.'

Through the silence, I could hear her brain whirring like a Mixmaster.

'I suppose that's that then,' she grudged. 'I don't know what your father will say.'

Poor Billy. We sat on the stiff lounge just feet away from Mum and Dad in their stiff chairs sipping their after-dinner coffees, watching Evonne Goolagong play Margaret Court at Wimbledon. Only our little fingers touched in the dark between us but the smell of him was in my nostrils and I wanted to hold him close.

When the game finished, my parents turned off the television and bricked up the fire. It was time for bed and there were no exceptions. I walked Billy to the front gate, where we stood close and kissed quickly in the dark.

'Dianne!' came the call from the house. 'Come in now.'

'Coming.'

I watched him in his big duffle coat as he walked up the street, waiting for him to turn and wave. He was going home to his mum and gran and brothers and sisters, where the kids rumbled and yelled and sat with their legs thrown over the arm of the chair. I wanted to go with him. I wanted their kitchen to become my kitchen, where I could drink cups of tea with his grandmother, chiack the smaller kids, and we could ruffle each other's hair and nobody would mind. Instead, I was staying here in the stony silence of our house expecting, at any moment, to be flayed by another chip splitting off.

9

After my wins with the golf club and Wimbledon, my mother regrouped and set in motion a campaign to make sure Billy didn't darken our doorstep again, literally and metaphorically.

She tried motherly concern. 'I just thought it would save you the walk if I picked you up,' she said when she appeared at the bus stop one afternoon. 'You must be tired and you'll be able to get your homework done sooner.'

Most days from then on, one of my parents would be waiting to drive me the couple of blocks to safety. I preferred to walk, not just in case I saw Billy but so I could get the smell of the little boys on the bus out of my nostrils: a mixture of sweat and sugary-sweet lollies.

She tried martyrdom. 'No, it's all right. Don't you worry about it,' she'd say when I offered to pop up to the shops to pick up the flour she'd forgotten. 'You just get on with your homework, that's far more important. I can do it. Thank you for offering, though.'

She tried the Arctic winter. If Billy rang, she was politely terse when she answered the phone but when our hands brushed as she handed it over, her eyes narrowed in line with her lips and I'd feel the start of the icy creep that would eventually work its way down the walls from the roof cavity. The thermometer would plummet for days.

When I managed to evade her ministrations and Billy drove me home, the mercury went the other way. Billy and I would sit in the car with the engine idling, just like all courting couples did in Coolamon. I didn't lean against him, like the other couples did, though. I kept my space, my eyes on alert for when my mother appeared on the front veranda, scowl in place, eyes dark.

'Dianne! It's time you came in. Now!'

As I walked into the house, she'd blast me with the heat of her fury. 'Good girls don't sit in cars,' she'd rage. 'You're turning into a tramp. You want to watch yourself, young lady. I've a good mind to get that strap out. That'll teach you.'

She didn't get it out, but I could see her palm itching.

The strap never came out again after she dragged me out of the pool away from Chris. Maybe she'd shocked herself that day as she thrashed and screamed. Maybe she frightened herself with her loss of control and it reminded her of her own mother.

Stories about Grandmother Whitby have come out patchily through my life and it wasn't until I was an adult that I realised what an interesting woman she had been. She had ten children and did a radio announcer course by correspondence and another one on cake decorating. When she received an inheritance from London of one hundred pounds, she gave it to the Rocky Hall hamlet to build the community hall that still stands today. When I blithely asked my mother and aunts and uncles for more memories of her, if they would write something or let me interview them, I started to understand how lucky Grandmother had been to have ten children – enough for at least some of them to love her while others were dismissive and resentful. Some were just sad.

'I'm sorry, love,' said Uncle Garnet, Mum's youngest brother, who rarely came to family get-togethers. 'I'm sorry I haven't sent you anything. I just couldn't do it. I tried. I tried a few times but every time I got out the paper and pen and sat down to write, I started to cry. I couldn't help it. Every time. It was like I could still see Mother with the belt in her hand, whipping John and Keith while they were in the bath. I could still see the welts rising on their wet skin. I just couldn't do it.'

My mother was my main source of information, becoming more and more willing as she aged to talk about her childhood and Grandmother Whitby.

'Things weren't very happy in our house,' she revealed. 'There wasn't much love around. Mother was harsh. The first time I went out at night, to a film, or a dance, I can't remember what it was, your grandmother met me inside the front door when I got home, with a stick in her hand, and belted me. She said it was in case I'd done something I shouldn't.'

My mother gave up the physical punishment earlier than her mother did, but then she had to find other ways to make sure I didn't do things I shouldn't.

When it became obvious to her that icy silences and red-hot frontal attacks didn't stop me wanting to be with Billy, she resorted to the woman-to-woman chat, attempting reason in the temperate zone. 'Here, Dianne, have a little break from your study,' she said as she came into my bedroom one weekend morning. 'I squeezed an orange juice for you.'

The morning breeze was billowing the curtains, riffling my pages, and the room was warm with the sun.

Mum stood next to my desk fiddling with her apron as I drank the juice. 'I want to talk to you,' she said, her voice heavy with faux concern. 'I don't want you to see Billy again. Don't get upset, but there's something not right with him, not right in the head. He's got a mental problem. Surely you can see that, and if you go on like this, you'll just be throwing your life away. One day you'll meet someone else, someone much more suitable, so forget about him now and concentrate on your schoolwork. It'll be for the best, you'll see.'

I sat in silence waiting for her to finish. Logarithmic equations zoomed in and out from the worksheet and the spire on the cover of William Golding's book wobbled, but I would not look at her.

'All right,' she said resignedly. 'I've said what I wanted to say and I hope you listened. I don't want any more of this nonsense. I'm sick of it. Do you understand me? Just do as I say. Don't encourage him. Now, get back to your homework, there's a good girl.'

She seemed to think that the way my heart responded to Billy was in my control. Maybe her heart had never ached for the glimpse of a particular boy; maybe she'd never felt such a rush of adrenalin when she did see him.

'Want to come to the drive-in with me tonight?' Billy asked one blistering afternoon as we chatted through the pool fence.

I'd been swimming and sunbaking most of the day while he'd been toiling in the paddocks. His navy-blue singlet, pungent with dust and sweat, reminded me of my father when I was a little girl. I'd loved crawling onto his lap for whiskered smooches before bed, the farm, the pub and the cigarettes mingling on his blue singlet to give him his particular Dad smell. I wanted to bury my nose in Billy's singlet too.

'Yeah, right,' I laughed. 'Much as I'd love to, I can't imagine that happening. I'll see you down at the basketball later, though.'

It was one of those golden evenings at the pool when the rising disc of the moon stretched orange across the horizon as it came up behind the bowling club. Mum had turned up with a chicken and salad picnic tea and Dad had come through from the club to join us. Neither of my parents ever swam: it was years since Mum had dog-paddled around, making sure her make-up didn't get wet, her hair tucked in a bathing cap, and I'd only ever seen Dad's grey swimming shorts balloon as he floated once or twice. Instead, my parents settled themselves onto the rug, in good moods because they were cooler than they'd been all day, and tea was served.

Billy's invitation was whirling around in my brain. I desperately wanted to go; I wanted to be like other girls who had boyfriends. Valda was allowed to go with Tony, so why couldn't I? I wanted to be a brave girl. If I didn't stand up for myself and for Billy now, I knew I might never get the opportunity again. I also knew that I was risking my parents' wrath just by asking but I took a deep breath.

'Um, Mum, Dad, I was wondering if I could go to the drive-in with Billy tonight.'

'Oh, Dianne!' Mum huffed, throwing down her fork, her face closing down with disgust. 'How can you even ask that? You know what we think. Why do you insist on bringing this up? I've told you to stay away from him.'

'Please, can I?'

Dad sat glowering, gnawing at a drumstick and not saying anything, his face getting redder by the second.

'I'm fed up with this. Why do you have to ruin our tea?' Mum continued. 'No, you can't go. I don't know why you're even asking. I tell you what, young lady, when we get home...'

'Oh, for goodness sake,' exploded Dad, throwing his bone into the Tupperware. 'Why don't we just let her? If she wants to throw her life away...'

'Ross!' Mum was aghast.

'Well, she's got to learn. Just let her go and be done with it. You seem hell bent on getting yourself into trouble, do you know that, missy? Well, go. I wash my hands of it. It's on your own head. You might trust him, but I certainly don't.'

'I do trust him, Dad. Honestly. He's always really good to me. He never...'

But Dad waved his arms. He didn't want to hear.

'But Ross,' sputtered Mum.

'No, let her go. She'll learn. I'm sick of all this business. Go on then. You might as well go now.'

My heart was pumping wildly as I quickly gathered my swim bag, towel and thongs. I wanted to leave before he changed his mind.

The picture that night was *There's a Girl in My Soup* with Peter Sellers and Goldie Hawn, but that's all I remember about it. We were alone, for hours, sitting close, but nothing happened, as we said in those days. We just kissed and I put my face against his T-shirt, breathing in his smell. His body was taut beneath the cotton. My hands wanted to feel his bare flesh – but Billy put them firmly back in my lap.

'No, no, no,' he laughed. 'Don't do that. You don't know where that might lead and I respect you too much.'

He respects me, I marvelled. That must mean he really likes me. That's what it means, doesn't it? That'll show my father.

I ached to tell Billy that I loved him – I wanted to tell everybody – but I was scared that he'd laugh at me and I didn't know what I'd do then.

We went once more to the drive-in, but secretly, aided and abetted by my friend Rhonda, who'd moved to town when her father took over the management of the Coolamon pub. They'd lived in Coolamon briefly a few years before and we'd become friends then, writing to each other after her family moved. Rhonda wasn't scared of my mother and she had a joking camaraderie with my father, who she saw at the pub every day. Plus, she liked Billy. Finally, I had an ally, someone I could actually say his name to, someone who didn't make fun of me.

Billy and Rhonda and I plotted in the poolroom at the pub, the only room we underage girls were allowed in. We roped in her older sister Sandra, and she took Rhonda and me to the drive-in, teaching us to do the drawback on the way. My first real cigarette – Helen's father's butts didn't count.

Billy went in another car with one of his mates. Once there, he and I were left alone. I don't even remember what this film was called, but again, nothing happened.

'None of that,' he laughed, when my hand, of its own volition, strayed down to his hips.

My body was yearning for something more but I didn't know what it was. I didn't think it could be sex. I was always shocked speechless when one of my friends said they'd done it, embarrassed that they even talked about it. A couple of them had written about it in their diaries and their mothers had read them. One mother had even arrived at school and taken her daughter home. They'd been in big trouble and, except for school, they were grounded forever. I couldn't believe they'd survived to tell the tale. I would save it for my wedding day. When I was with Billy, I wanted to melt into his bones, into his flesh, but I never thought about actually having sex.

The pedestal of respect was becoming very lonely, though. My insides ached even when I was close to him, and I couldn't get close enough. At the drive-in that night, I swung between joy and sadness. I wanted the film to never end.

True to form, our clandestine rendezvous was found out, but not by my mother or father. After seeing us go, Rhonda's mother had seen

Billy heading off to Wagga and she put two and two together. She was a woman of few words, Rhonda's mother, and none of them were scary.

'You've put me in a difficult position,' she grumbled when we got home. 'You girls shouldn't have done this. There'll only be trouble. I know what your parents think, Dianne. I won't tell them this time, but don't do it again.'

As it turned out, the opportunity never came. Billy's life had started to spiral out of control when he got his driver's licence. He went everywhere at speed, except when I was in the car. One night, as our family was puttering home in our distinctive mushroom-and-white Holden station wagon after dinner at Mama and Pa's, we had just bumped over the railway crossing when lights suddenly appeared from the crossroad to our right, barrelling down upon us at full speed out of the darkness. Dad slammed on the brakes and a car tore through the intersection in front of us. In the brief flash of a streetlight, I saw that it was Billy behind the wheel.

'Bloody fool,' Dad growled.

Nobody else said anything; I just wanted to cry. He had surely just nailed shut any possibility of my parents accepting him, and I worried that he would be the next young Coolamon bloke to end up in the cemetery.

'What are you worried about?' he'd laugh. 'I'll be all right. And what would it matter anyway?'

'It would matter to me,' I'd say.

As his risk-taking behaviour increased, my life was changing too, but in a separate sphere. I was making new friends at Wagga High and having different experiences. One of my new friends, Julie, had a weekend sleepover at her place when her mother was working night shift at the hospital and I heard Bob Dylan's 'Lay Lady Lay' for the first time. Janet, who'd been to boarding school and smoked in front of her parents, and Marg, whose hair was almost as long as her legs, drank Julie's mother's beer that was kept in the back of the fridge to use as shampoo. I was shocked. When an unsteady and raucous Janet peed into the empty bottle, I wanted to cry. Instead, I walked off alone into the dark.

I was learning new things in school too.

'What does copulate mean?' I asked Miss Atwell, our level one English teacher, when Chaunticleer copulated with Pertelote in 'The Nun's Priest Tale'.

Helen didn't know either but everybody else in the class laughed at us.

I learnt about Mao's *Little Red Book* from the boy who they said smoked pot and, when one of the girls became pregnant, I watched in amazement as her tummy grew and she kept coming to school.

I started going to Wagga on the weekends as well: my new friends had roped me into playing on their hockey team on Saturday afternoons, and I joined the cheer squad for the Wagga High rugby league team. The twenty-five miles there and twenty-five miles back accumulated, taking me further and further away from Coolamon in body and mind, and further away from the life I thought I wanted to have with Billy.

I kept looking for him every day: he was the only boy who set my pulse racing and I still hoped that we could be together. I didn't care that everyone thought he was a lout: I liked the Coolamon louts. They may have been rough and always in trouble with the police sergeant but they were nice to me and I felt safe around them. Maybe I was naïve, but I didn't believe it was any of the boys who waved to me who did the things with girls behind the shops at night that Billy told me about.

Billy didn't tell me everything, though. That was left to Rhonda.

'Billy's having sex with other girls,' she told me.

The same girls who threw me dagger looks, the ones who were allowed to do whatever they wanted, like hang around with boys at night. It felt like the farm scarifier was raking across my heart, tearing it to pieces. With each rip, I thought about how my parents could say 'I told you so.' I thought about all the pitying looks I managed not to see. I thought about how everybody knew except me. I thought about how I wasn't good enough to have sex with.

That's why he never touched me, I thought. He just said he respected me to make it easy. He's probably laughing at me too.

Under the bedclothes at night, I sobbed my heart out.

'Are you sure you're all right, Dianne?' Mum asked me in the mornings. 'You look washed-out. Are you studying too hard, do you think? Do you need to take a day off?'

'I'm fine, Mum. Just a bit tired.'

I didn't want it to be the end, even though I knew deep down that it would never work out: he'd left school at fifteen and I was hoping to go to university; he was Catholic and I was Presbyterian and that still mattered in Coolamon; and even though he lived on our side of town, just around the corner and down the street, my family thought he was from the wrong side of the tracks.

I knew it must have been all my fault so, instead of hating him, I hated myself. I hated my body and what people saw when they looked at me. I hated the inside of my head. I hated the aching in my heart. I couldn't be angry with him because I didn't have any right to be: that would be assuming he'd promised me something and he hadn't.

Helen had given me a five-year diary for Christmas and I distilled my pain into the four lines available for each day of the year. Stupid, fat and ugly featured prominently. Every night I prayed – Please God, Please God – and every day my diary says 'saw Billy today' or 'didn't see Billy today'.

When I did see him, he was just the same. He'd look at me with his deep dark eyes and hold my gaze until any resolve I had to ignore him faded away.

Maybe it was all a mistake; maybe Rhonda was wrong.

But I knew she wasn't and sometimes, when we ended up in each other's company at Rhonda's pub or at the pool, and after his smiles and tenderness had worn me down, I tried to talk to him about what was happening, to tell him how sad I was.

'Hey,' he'd laugh, 'don't be sad. The world's not ending tomorrow.'

'Just be serious for a change, can you?' I told him at the pool one day.

He stopped joshing and looked at me. 'Darling, I love you,' he said. The air around me stilled. He had said it. But did he mean it? He was probably just mucking around.

'Yeah, yeah,' I replied, stunned and cautious.

'You've got me and I've got you,' he said when he gave me a lift home another day.

I didn't reply. I couldn't. I didn't trust that he wasn't making fun of me.

Then, suddenly, whatever it was between us was over. One of the girls he had sex with became pregnant and that was that. I felt humiliated, ashamed that I hadn't been enough for him and that everyone would now know that he preferred her to me. I slunk around town, trying to remain invisible. And still I was angry with myself: angry that I couldn't change the way I felt about him. I knew I had to, though: a baby was serious.

The girl who was having his baby hated me like nobody else ever had. 'Stupid fucking bitch,' she swore at me when we ran into each other at a football game. 'Why don't you just fuck off!'

That's what his family wanted me to do too. They took her under their wing, as was right, and the chill that came off them when they saw me turned me to an icicle.

A few months later, Billy and I had one final stolen afternoon together. I was staying in Wagga with Marg in the summer holidays and strolling down Wagga's main street one day we ran into Johnny. He and Marg had started flirting when she'd stayed at my place. Billy was with him and we stood looking at each other as the other two arranged to go for a swim. The boys knew a good spot on the Murrumbidgee and, because it was a peaceful weekday, nobody would be around. The sun was shining and it was hot with just the hint of a gentle breeze. Billy and I were left alone and swam in the river, diving down to touch the slushy mud on the bottom and hanging on to the roots at the bank, letting the current waft us about. When we'd had enough of that, we sat on our towels in the shade of the trees. It was so quiet nothing else existed. Even the birds were holding their breath.

'How've you been? How's school going?'

'Yeah, good. Lots of work. What about you? Are you still working for Moses?'

We didn't mention the other girl.

We sat close, drawing in the dirt, laughing at our stick figures. Our hands found each other and we let our fingers play.

'I'm sorry,' he said.

'Me too,' I said.

I could feel the caress of the breezes on my belly and back, and on this lovely summer's day, for perhaps the first time ever, I felt beautiful.

10

Please God, I prayed, don't let my mother know about Billy. I don't want to deal with her I-told-you-so glee.

My parents dug the spade in occasionally to see what they came up with.

'That young Marshall,' my father would grumble, 'he's going to run into a lot of trouble one day.'

They'd both peer at me to see my reaction but I ignored them, pretending I hadn't heard and had no interest anyway, pretending there wasn't a huge ache where my heart had been. Eventually they gave up, and Billy's name was never mentioned in our house again – ever.

My mother moved her attentions elsewhere then. She'd been trying to stuff me in a box of her own making, with a too-tight lid and a neat red ribbon tied in a bow since I was born but I kept bouncing out, upsetting her plans. I didn't know that those plans extended to my girlfriends as well as my boyfriends. Her lips had always shrunk together whenever Billy was mentioned. Now they started shrinking when Helen's name came up.

'You're always going there. She never comes here. You just crawl to her. What's wrong with you? You need to get your head screwed on straight, young lady.'

She was right: Helen never came to our house, but why would she want to? I didn't want to be there either. I wanted to be with her, though, and was always inviting her to come to the pictures or to the river or to a barbecue out at the farm, but she never came. Not once. In hindsight, she wasn't going anywhere much at all, withdrawing from all activities, but at the time I thought it was just part of our dance and it was me she didn't want to be around. And as usual, the more withdrawn she became, the more desperately I chased after her.

'Haven't you got homework to do?'

My mother's voice would follow me up the hall as I crept out of the house. I knew that if I didn't go to Helen, she wouldn't come to me, and what would that mean about our friendship? I refused to let her go. There was too much history: the steps we cut into the paddock, the boring afternoons, the cemetery, the wet-your-pants laughs, the sleepovers, the Purple Pinkie Club.

With no idea about what was happening for her, I would convince myself that she was being aloof because she hated me, and I'd try to stay away. See how she likes that, I'd think. I'll show her I don't need her. If she wants to see me, then she can come to me.

The sun would keep rising and setting and I'd hang out with Marianne or Deirdre but, always, after a week or so, I'd buckle and creep back to her side. I needed to be near her to keep my squirming anxiety at bay.

When we started in fifth form at Wagga High, we took with us the pattern of our childhood. We came as a pair: like Fred and Ginger, Sonny and Cher, Hels and Di. We were Muscles and Spook, a silly name invented by my teasing Coolamon classmates – Spookus Lucas. We shared classes, desks, and new friends. We sat together on the school bus even when she wasn't speaking to me. Each morning, I waited to see what mood she was in, whether she liked me that day or not, before attempting to talk. It was usually a quiet trip and I spent my time staring out the window, scanning the trucks and paddocks for a glimpse of Billy's black curls, my personal tarot card: if I saw them, my day would likely go well. More often than not, I had to be satisfied with a dead tree.

I'd always found the land around Coolamon tedious with the long straight roads heading off into the wavy distance and the flat paddocks stretching to the horizon. I didn't know then that the haystacks dotted over those paddocks were almost unique to our area and I never bothered noticing the brush growing along the roads. I liked the trees in our street – the cedars with their tiny sticky pods that I used to serve my doll for dinner, the kurrajongs and their tough black pods full of filmy seeds, and the purple jacarandas – but I thought the trees in the bush were just the same messy scrub as around the cemetery. And then one day, when the last hope of seeing Billy had vanished, I fell in love with a tree. It was long dead but that didn't matter: its silvery-smooth trunk arched up, becoming two strong branches that stretched into the sky, reaching for something out of their grasp. Every morning, my eyes swept up its length to the sky, my back arching and stretching with it, searching and yearning for something I couldn't reach either.

'Good morning, tree,' I'd whisper.

'What's so special about that tree?' asked Helen one day. 'It's dead.'

'Dunno. It's just my marker for the first lap,' I replied.

Helen liked my idea of breaking the journey into laps and, on the days when she was talking to me, we breathed together.

Two, when we picked up Bronwyn Hamilton.

Three, as we let our bodies roll with the sweep of the deep S-bend at the halfway mark.

Four, when we leant into the nasty bend at Houlaghans Creek.

Five, at the top of the hill where we saw the new yellow crop for the first time. 'It's called rape,' the big boys tittered, but I didn't believe them.

Six, as the bus gave way at Cartwright's Hill T-junction, and seven, as we crossed Hampton Bridge over the Murrumbidgee, which sometimes flooded at North Wagga and stopped the bus getting through to our school on the hill.

Regardless of what our day had been like, I never thought of not sitting with Helen on the trip home. I knew she wasn't really herself. We'd always had our ups and downs and she, maybe rightfully, thought I was an idiot a lot of the time but, since we went on that last Purple Pinkie diet together, something had changed. She could be quite snappy, sometimes even nasty, and she tucked herself in like an echidna, the spikes warning me off. I didn't know what was happening, but I felt very protective of her.

There were good days when we'd laugh all the way home, especially when Bobby Allen, our bus driver, made us share our seat in his swish new bus with a little boy who liked licking the windows. There was no laughing, though, when Bobby accused Helen and me of biting the headrest of the seat in front of us.

'What a dickhead! As if we'd do that.'

'Who does he think we are? How old does he think we are?'

'Maybe he's only joking.'

But he wasn't, and he threatened to split us up. We didn't say good morning to him for a whole week.

Most of the time, though, Helen spoke to me in monosyllables and I became accustomed to her silences and scathing looks when I'd… when I'd… Well, when I didn't know what I'd done.

'Your neck must be getting pretty sore,' she'd scoff when I craned around to talk to Marianne in the seat behind us.

Some days, I hardly dared breathe because I annoyed her so much, and I took extra care to make sure I didn't take up too much space. But, always, at the first sign of her softening, I was ready to forgive.

One afternoon, after a day of dodging her ground-to-air missiles, we walked out of Iverach's shop together.

'I don't know what happens to me,' she said, suddenly. 'I want to be nice to you but it's like something just takes over my brain and I'm horrible.'

I looked at her quickly to see if she was joking but she didn't seem to be. I was aware that I needed to get this next bit right and my pulse beat faster.

'Mmm, well…yeah,' was what came out of my mouth. 'Like a monster in your head?'

'I hate it. It makes me say all those nasty things. I don't want to but I can't stop it. It is a monster.'

'Well, it's not really you then, is it? So, when it happens,' I suggested, 'let's call her Agnes.'

Not that I ever dared to actually use that name: if Agnes was out and about, I kept my mouth shut, but it was reassuring to know that she didn't really despise me.

She didn't like my mother, though, and surprisingly, while I could understand it, that hurt. I didn't want my mother disdained, picked over and found wanting by others. I was protective of her too, even though she made my life miserable, and even though I often wished she wasn't my mother.

My teenage years would have been particularly difficult for Mum, especially since they started in the sixties when Bob Dylan was singing about the times achanging, and the Rolling Stones were singing so blatantly about sex. Everything she clung on to as decent, moral and ladylike was challenged: Jean Shrimpton came to the Melbourne Cup in a miniskirt and no hat; Twiggy was on every magazine cover with a boy's short haircut; and, on television, couples, married or not, started sleeping in the same bed. There was the Vietnam War, student riots in France, and students being shot on an American university campus. And everywhere, young people wanted to make love, not war.

Helen had always thought my mother was mean because we were only allowed to have one, or at the most two, biscuits, and her homemade ice cream came in a small sliver. I didn't know how to explain to her, or even appreciate myself, that Mum was one of ten kids in a family living through the Depression and the Second World War and that she wasn't mean, she was just the Queen of Frugality and her life was devoted to making ends meet. She even started saving Gladwrap when it was invented.

I didn't know enough then to describe what it must have been like for my mother, who looked so radiant and hopeful on her wedding day, to discover that my father didn't like women much and the income on his tax return was usually nil. From the outside, we looked like the average middle-class Coolamon family but it was a sham: Mum was paddling fiercely to put food onto the table while Dad cruised off to the pub every spare moment, to spend his coins on beer.

My new Wagga friends didn't have any preconceived ideas about who

I was, who my family was, or what my mother was like, and they embraced me as much as Helen. They laughed at my jokes and invited me to their houses; they never teased me about my big lips, or my big nose, or my frizzy hair. Their warmth made me feel like I was a real person, not just somebody else's sidekick. When Helen wasn't with me, I no longer panicked about what to say and what people might think. My Coolamon skin began to work itself free. It had started puckering when it was obvious there was no future for Billy and me and it wrinkled and loosened further as I spent more and more time away from the town, escaping my parents but also the people up the main street who had always known it could never work out between Billy and me. I stayed for days on end in Wagga with my Great-Aunty Doreen, Mama's sister, going to school, playing hockey, and rehearsing for the play, *The Diary of Anne Frank* – I was Mrs Van Danne, Helen was Anne, and we tied first place in the Riverina Drama Festival. I also started going out with a boy from one of the other high schools.

Our gang of girls had been sitting on Wagga High's grassy hillside during lunchtime one day, when a car of Mount Austin boys stopped illegally at the kerb and a very tall golden-haired boy jumped out, leapt the fence and ran up the slope towards us. He stopped in front of me.

'Would you like to come out with me some time?' he panted. 'Could I have your phone number?'

I'd never seen him before, but he obviously knew who I was. I didn't want to be rude so I gave him my number. It didn't take long: Coolamon 52.

He ran back down the hill while his mates whooped and hollered, and the boys he knew from our school whooped and hollered too. I sat red-faced, giggling with my friends, while everybody else stared.

Ken was very attentive, driving out to see me in Coolamon, introducing me to his family, giving me flowers, but I wasn't a very good girlfriend. I liked him a lot but he didn't make my pulse race like Billy did. Nobody ever would, probably.

I wasn't planning on staying around either. I dreamed of leaving Coolamon. I wanted to let my skin loose where nobody had any ideas about me. I wanted to get away from my parents and from being a Lucas as well. My grandmother wanted me in the same box, with the same red ribbon around it, as my mother did, and Mama never held back her criticism either, although not always to my face.

My loyal brother Paul always reported back to me. 'Mama said you're getting too big for your boots. Mama said you looked like a tramp in your jeans and T-shirt.'

There had been good times with Mama when we'd nestled down in the twin beds in the girls' room and chatted into the wee hours of the morning about what happened when Edward VIII had abdicated, what Wallis Simpson was really like, how sad it was for Queen Elizabeth when her father died, and how Princess Margaret wasn't allowed to marry the love of her life – my further education in kings and queens and sealing wax.

Mostly, though, she sniffed her nose at me and pursed her lips, scanning me from top to toe. 'Why you don't wear the pretty dresses your mother makes I'll never know,' she grumbled when I wore jeans. 'You should be ashamed of yourself, young lady, wearing that short dress,' she'd hiss at other times. 'I don't know what your mother was thinking, letting you come out like that. And look at your hair!'

'No, Mama,' I'd say. 'I don't want to use rollers or always have my hair in plaits. Yes, Mama, I know it's frizzy.'

There was nothing to make me want to stay in Coolamon but I didn't know what I wanted to do or where I wanted to go. I only knew that I wanted to be like the students I'd seen on American campuses clutching folders to their chests. I wanted to sit down in the street with the students on the news and sing for a world without war. Mr Padovan would have approved of that. He'd opened my eyes to all that was wrong with the Vietnam War and then there was the little Vietnamese girl running and burning. My brother was just lucky that his marble didn't come up but Dianne Bell's uncle and Valda's brother both went, farewelled by the town at a supper tea in the RSL Hall, and they'd both come back different, a lot sadder. I wanted to be a part of stopping that.

Nursing was a possibility. I could go with Helen, but just the thought of the boil on my father's back that Mum had to clean and dress made me want to retch. I couldn't do that. A secretary, then: I'd wanted to be one of those once when I saw a film where secretaries carried shoulder bags, but nowadays anybody could have a shoulder bag. When I was in primary school and looked after the cute little kindergarten kids, I wanted to be a teacher, but having seen how older kids treated teachers, that was off my list too. The school vocational guidance counsellor analysed my answers to a questionnaire and suggested I could be a librarian or a journalist. I didn't know anything about journalism and while it sounded exciting, it also sounded scary. I knew about books, though: they would keep me safe.

There was a librarianship course available in Canberra close to my Whitby aunts and uncles. My parents approved. A few weeks after my future was decided, we drove through Canberra to a family gathering, passing a grand building soaring up beside the lake. It resembled one of the old Greek buildings that was now a ruin. The banner unfurled down its side proclaimed it to be the National Library.

'I'm going to work there one day,' I said, admiring its classic columns. 'I'm going to be the head librarian.'

'Really, dear?' My parents threw amused looks at each other and laughed.

11

Within the space of a couple of weeks in December 1972, my life changed forever.

For a start, on the first Saturday of the month, and after twenty-three years, the Labor Party won a federal election. This was the first time I'd taken any notice of an election campaign. Not because I was interested in the politics but because Little Pattie, Jackie Weaver and Jack Thompson were singing about how it was time for a change. On past election days, the fun had been in going to our school on a weekend, sitting with Helen behind an Australian flag draped over the grass, and arranging the coins thrown down for the Red Cross around the stripes of the Union Jack. This year I was too busy to do that: I was packing to go to Canberra the next day.

My parents were up voting when there was a knock at the door. I was taken aback when I saw Chris standing on our front veranda. I'd hardly dared look at him since my mother had pulled me out of the pool by my ear.

He'd come to say goodbye. 'It was fun when we were going together,' he said.

'Mmm,' I agreed, as my chest filled with delight. I hadn't known we had been.

Billy was on the veranda that day too, standing back, and I didn't see him straight away. My heart lurched when he came into view and I did a quick prayer that my parents wouldn't come home right then. As the three of us leaned against the veranda railing, chatting and reminiscing like old friends do, I felt a warm glow settle around me and a stirring of excitement in my gut: it was all going to be okay.

Billy gave me a farewell present that day: a small gold cross set with a red stone. When we'd been almost-going-together, and I was away on holidays, he'd bought me a cross with a blue stone. He'd told me about it when I came home, how another girl had seen it and claimed it. I thought he'd just said that, and had given it to her because he liked her better.

'This one is for you,' he said.

I still have it.

The next day, I gazed steadfastly out the car window as Mum and Dad drove me out of Coolamon, past the crisping paddocks and through dusty towns lying in wait to see what the summer had in store. A confusion of anticipation and terror made me want to burst into tears. But I couldn't do that. Over the years, my resolve not to cry in front of my mother had only hardened. Just the thought of her trying to comfort me made me squirm, and I didn't want to deal with her emotions either.

'It feels like we're in for a hot summer,' offered Mum.

'Yep,' said Dad, twisting his neck away from his collar in the way he did, trying to escape the stiffness.

'How are you feeling, Dianne? Do you need some pineapple?'

My mother always travelled with a Tupperware container of canned pineapple pieces: it was good for nausea apparently, and I was renowned for getting carsick.

'I'm fine, thanks.' I wondered if she was thinking about when she'd left home.

'Your grandmother kicked me out,' she'd told me.

'What? Why?' I'd asked, stunned.

'I'd become a bit of a rebel, I suppose.'

When pressed, she'd admitted becoming resentful at having to do so much for Grandmother's shop. She'd become sullen and uncooperative and Grandmother told her to leave. She'd caught a train to Sydney, where her sisters, Winnie and Elsie, were nursing.

'I only lasted a week,' she continued. 'I stayed at the YWCA in the city and it was too noisy. The traffic. So I went back home to Queanbeyan. Mother wasn't pleased to see me. She turned me around, gave me five pounds and a suitcase, and told me to send them both back.'

There was no danger of the Canberra traffic noise sending me scurrying home. Everywhere was eerily quiet, not like a proper city. Dad didn't have to curse the traffic at all as we came into town and we could have driven through the red lights on the main drag without mishap. I hadn't expected such stillness, or the deserted streets. There wasn't even any rubbish blowing in the gutters. As we drove past the uniformly drab two-storey buildings. I wondered if Gough and Margaret were on their way to Canberra that day too. I know now that, when they did arrive, a few days after me, the Lodge hadn't been ready for them, just like my room at the Macquarie Private Hotel hadn't been ready for me.

When I'd walked into the foyer of the sprawling red-brick building that was to be my new home, I was almost exploding with excitement. Ever since we'd left Coolamon, I'd been imagining the moment when I'd settle into my room, say goodbye to my parents, and my new life would begin. I held back a whimper as I followed my parents back outside again: my hopes had been kicked into a ditch.

'You'd think they'd have things better organised than this,' grumbled my mother as we drove back over Commonwealth Bridge to a temporary room at Ursula College, a student residence run by nuns at the Australian National University. 'I hope you'll be all right, Dianne.'

'Hmmm. Makes you wonder what we pay our taxes for,' groused Dad. 'She'll be all right, though, as long as the nuns don't mess with her head.'

'Oh, Ross. Don't say that.'

The nuns were the least of their worries.

I was alone for the first time in seventeen and a half years, and I was lonely immediately. There was nothing to soften the impact of landing in a strange room that was only slightly bigger than our laundry at home, a room that might have suited a nun with its narrow bed, veneer cupboard and small square of desk, but I felt abandoned. There were no cheerful curtains, no welcoming rug, just a cloud of depression hovering near the ceiling, and the faint scent of other lonely strangers. I wish, now, that I'd taken the pink chenille bedspread from my bed at home, or even the tinsel dome with the broken-tailed fish, but I hadn't known then that you can make a space your own, that you can decorate a room to reflect who you are. Besides, those things belonged to my parents' house, not to me.

I hung up my few dresses, opened my beauty case and arranged the toothpaste and mascara on the desk. Then I had nothing to do except listen to the ringing silence. I sat awkwardly on the thin mattress, my hands under my legs, gazing at the only adornment in the room, a small picture of Jesus on the cross. He made me feel sad but it was only mid-afternoon and there were hours to go before I could crawl under the serviceable brown bedcover and lose myself in sleep. I knew I would have to leave the room eventually, that I should at least pretend I knew what I was doing, so I willed myself to turn the doorknob. There wasn't a nun in sight; nobody, in fact. All the students who lived there must have gone back to their homes for summer holidays, and here I was, travelling the other way. I crept downstairs and scuttled out the front door. I didn't know what I'd say if anyone did appear.

I headed off through the deserted campus in what I hoped was the direction of the city centre. It was hot, and I thought how in Coolamon I'd be at the pool by now. I walked until I came upon the main avenue we'd driven down when we came into town. It was as quiet as Coolamon's main street on a Sunday. I didn't notice the hills rising to the east and west, nor the leafy green trees. I was only aware of being out of place, awkwardly self-conscious and embarrassed that the people in the few passing cars would think nobody wanted to be with me. I wandered past some closed shops, feigning interest in the window displays – the silver watches in Prouds Jewellers, the rings in Emmets, the clothes mannequins in Katies – but really, I was using the glass as a mirror to see if anything was going on around me. Nothing was.

As I headed back to Ursula College, scared to go too far afield, I noticed a pub on the corner of Northbourne Avenue. I peeked in its front door to see if it was like the Coolamon pubs. It wasn't. There was no lino to be seen but right in front of me was a cigarette machine. I'd never bought a packet of cigarettes before, except when I went up to the newsagent to buy Dad his unfiltered Phillip Morris. I fished around in my purse and found enough change to buy a packet of Winfield Reds. They were cheap, and 'Anyhow, have a Winfield' had been Ken's favourite ad when we were dating. A bartender hoisting bottles from a back room to a gloomy bar sold me a box of matches and I carried my booty back to my room, proud of my first away-from-home decision. To celebrate, I lit up. My head started spinning, my stomach curdled, and my mouth tasted like I'd licked an ashtray, but I persevered, hopeful that this would be my entry point to an independent future.

The next evening, after my first day of work at the Commonwealth Electoral Office, where I'd sat counting pieces of paper from some of the voting booths, I took another step towards sophistication. I'd always wanted to be one of those young women whose hair swayed sleekly as she rode a horse along the beach and, five years after I'd first tried, I was determined to use a tampon. Surely, I reasoned, now that I know there's another hole down there, it will be easy.

I sat in one of the toilets, listening to the laughter of girls in a room near mine, and tried again, pushing and manipulating until, finally, the little tube seemed to be in place. I walked back to my room flushed and happy.

'Hey, come in here,' one of the girls called. 'What's your name?'

They were girls like me from country towns, lured to Canberra as part of a vacation employment scheme in the Public Service, a way station between school and university, or, for me, a degree in librarianship at the relatively new Canberra College of Advanced Education. I don't remember any boys recruited in the same way. Maybe they were expected to keep the country towns and farms going.

They fired questions at me. 'Where are you from? What department are you working in? Are you excited?' They were mostly a daggy lot: a bit too earnest and eager, their skirts a bit long at the knee, their hair too smoothly pinned. I didn't want to be like them, so I was reserved in my answers.

Suddenly, the nun's intercom system burst into the room. 'Telephone call for Dianne Lucas. Dianne Lucas, telephone call. Long distance.'

'That's me,' I startled, surprised to hear my name so loudly in the air. 'Where's the phone?'

'Come on, I'll show you,' offered Carolyn, the girl with the long blonde hair and smiling eyes, the least daggy one there. 'Quick, it's on this floor but right around the other side. We'll have to run or they'll think you're not here and hang up.'

Before I turned the first corner, I knew something was amiss: with every step a spear jabbed through my insides. Carolyn kept on running and I loped after her wincing and clenching my teeth. When we reached the phone, my legs were splayed and I was doubled over with knife-thrusts of pain.

Carolyn watched me worriedly as I managed to make the right noises to satisfy my mother and hung up. 'What's wrong? You're all sweaty? Are you sick?'

'No,' I gasped. 'I tried to use a tampon but it's killing me. It's my first time. It mustn't be in right.'

'Come on,' she said, giggling, 'come to the loo and I'll help you.'

I stumbled into a cubicle while she ran off to grab another tampon.

'Right, can you get that one out? Squat down a bit, that'll help. Okay, now, sit on the toilet, spread your legs, and push it up, a bit backwards, and up. Up. Is that better?'

Carolyn became my new best friend.

At work, a couple of days later, I received a phone call to tell me I could move to the Macquarie hostel that evening. When I saw Carolyn, she'd had the same phone call. We would be moving together. Looking back, it would probably have been better if we'd both stayed at Ursula's.

To our delight, we were put in a room together in the special corridor for girls under eighteen. It was the only sign that anybody at Macquarie acknowledged or cared about our still under-age welfare. They didn't care enough, though, and Carolyn and I soon joined the evening exodus of twenty-somethings to the Wellington pub, just a block away.

The Wello wasn't like the Coolamon pubs either. While it was definitely a man's place, ladies were welcome in both of its bars, and instead of formica there was lots of dark wood, padded chairs, low coffee tables and pictures on the walls. By the end of the night, though, the floors were still beer-sticky, just carpet instead of lino.

I'd never liked the taste of alcohol when I was growing up. Just the smell of Dad's beer was enough to curl my nose, and when I was offered a glass of wine at Mama's family dinners, I was prim and righteous. 'No, thank you,' I'd say. 'I think it's disgusting.'

When I went to Wagga High and my friends took me to the Kooringal pub, far enough away from the centre of Wagga to feel safe from the prying eyes of parents or police, I'd discovered that Coca-Cola was good for hiding the taste of alcohol. I sat nursing one Bacardi and Coke, quietly aghast when my friends got a bit pissed. I was the good, sensible one who kept sober, who could provide cover with parents if necessary.

The first night at the Wello, after more than the usual Bacardi and Cokes, I discovered that I liked the feeling of being happy and slightly giddy in the middle of the crowd, and, even better, I didn't have to worry about getting into trouble when I arrived home. I didn't like it so much when my new best friend met a bloke and arranged to go out with him the next night.

As soon as they left for their date, my insides felt hollow. Everybody knew that if you were alone on a Friday night, then you were obviously a loser. I might as well be back in Coolamon. I had nowhere to be and nobody to be with. Panic bubbled up my throat. My life had been reduced to this small room with its four walls, two single beds and not much else. My head started to spin and I sat down on the bed, gripping the cheap brown and yellow striped bedspread to steady myself. I counted the red bricks in the wall above Carolyn's bed, starting again each time I lost count. The distraction didn't help.

'Nobody cares about you,' the bricks tittered. 'You're nothing,' they taunted.

I covered my ears to block them out but the jeering was inside my head.

'Think you're so grown-up, do you? But look at you – you're too scared to go out by yourself.'

The fear of being alone with the voices in the ugly, little room overcame my fear of being alone outside in the world, so I took my next step towards independence: I grabbed my bag, shut the door, and left the building. I only knew one place to go, though: the Wello.

I'd envied my father's escape to the pub every day. I'd wanted to sit with him, and the other men in their grease-encrusted King Gees, and discuss matters of consequence. I didn't want to wear a prissy apron and discuss a new recipe for scones or how Mrs Brown's daughter's husband's aunty had stopped going to church. I didn't want to drink tea from a delicate cup: my fingers wouldn't fit through the handles anyway. And now was my chance, even if the greasy overalls were replaced by clean and tidy public service leisurewear, jeans and T-shirts.

I perched on a stool, aware of the men's bodies leaning against the bar near me, the buzz of their conversation. With a drink in one hand, and a cigarette in the other, I tried to appear cool and confident, as if I was an old hand at going to a pub alone. I discovered that girls in the pub didn't talk to other girls who were by themselves, but the blokes did.

'Where are you from? Where's that? I'm from the country too. From Dubbo. Couldn't wait to get out of the place.'

'Don't listen to him. He's from Cootamundra. They don't know what they're talking about in Cootamundra, do ya, Rosco?'

'Have another? What are you drinking?'

'Here, have one of mine.'

Click, goes the lighter. I was having a wonderful time. My drinking companions were all from the hostel, and a couple of them were cute in a soft-cheeked way, not my type, though, whatever that was. The more I drank, the looser my limbs felt and I swayed and giggled as I made my way to the toilet. Then it was closing time and my new friends were heading off to a party.

'Come with us. There's plenty of room.'

'Nah. Better not.'

'I'll walk back with you,' offered John, a short, stocky bloke who'd stood on the edge of the group staring into his beer most of the night. 'I'm having an early night myself.'

'Oh, okay.' My head swirled and I stared hard at the path to keep my steps straight. Laughter bubbled up for no reason. I clutched at John's arm to steady myself. It was a long block that night between the pub and the hostel. I couldn't wait to lie down.

I came to sometime later in a dark room with someone on top of me. My head was spinning, or it could have been the room itself. I tried to get up but my shoulders were being held down. I was sure I was going to vomit. As my head cleared a little, I realised it was John making the strange grunting noises and there was a hard pressure between my legs. What was he trying to do? Panic surged through me and I lurched up, pushing him off. My blood snap-froze when I realised my dress was up around my waist and my underpants were hanging off one foot. Shaking with cold, I hoiked up my pants, pulled down my dress, grabbed my bag that was lying on the floor and reeled out the door.

'Where are you going? Hey, you! Come back.'

I stumbled down one deserted corridor after another, trying to find mine, the one with the A next to the room numbers on the door, the one that was specially to keep young girls like me safe. I needed a bathroom. When I sat for a wee, I couldn't feel anything below my waist. My legs were heavy to move and the rest of me was shaking like I was outside naked in the middle of winter. My gut recoiled from the thought that John had been trying to have sex with me, that the pressure I'd felt was him trying to get inside me. Thank God I'd woken up. I didn't want to think about what it would have meant if he'd managed it. I felt sick enough.

The next day passed in a blur. I sought the oblivion of sleep, an escape from the ominous shadow that hovered when I was awake.

Carolyn didn't come back all day and, when sleep exhausted itself, it was just the four brick walls and me – again.

The jeering voices were even louder tonight. 'Loser! they carped. 'Stupid! You made a fool of yourself. You'll be lucky if anyone wants to be friends with you.'

'You did make some friends last night,' a little voice whispered. 'They seemed nice, didn't they?'

I'd felt good being at the pub. It had been fun. I didn't feel good in this room with its taunting walls and loneliness

I could go there and just not drink as much, I reasoned, and not talk to that John fellow.

Saturday nights at pubs were always quieter than Friday nights, because most people had other places to go. Some of my buddies from the previous night were there, though, and welcomed me like I was part of their gang.

'Hey, what are you drinking? You missed a good party last night.'

I was bright and sparkly, laughing hard at their jokes, hoping they wouldn't leave me alone. Then John walked in. All my senses were alert to him as he stood at the bar sipping his beer. I prayed he didn't see me, and if he did, that he wouldn't come near me.

His eyes were sweeping the room and settled on me. He smirked and wandered over to our group, shouldering his way into its centre. 'Hello, darling,' he leered at me. 'Come back for seconds, have you?'

My stomach tightened into a ball and the previous night's big freeze descended again. I wanted to leave but I couldn't move.

He thrust out his chest and raised himself on his toes, pointing at me. 'Hey,' he called out to the room. 'Hey, everyone. I broke her!'

The hum and laughter in the room missed a beat, embarrassed looks were thrown towards me. People turned back to their friends, but seemed slightly toned down.

'She's a good screw, fellas,' he sneered to my gang. 'You're a stupid one, though. You left blood on my bed. The cleaner's not going to be impressed with that. That's for sure.' He looked me up and down then turned and left. 'See ya, fellows.'

The others shuffled their feet and coughed into their beers. My throat was clamped shut and I couldn't blink. There was a loud buzzing in my head.

One of the men put his arm around me. 'Don't worry love. It'll be all right. Do you want another drink? Anyone else for another? Your shout, Alan.'

My body had shut down but my brain was whirling. Wasn't I a virgin any more? How could I have not known? I didn't know it could happen so quickly, and so silently. I'd been holding on to it like it was a precious gem and now I hadn't even noticed the moment of its loss. I stood like a pillar of concrete in a raging wind: people swirled around me, buying drinks, feigning heartiness, pretending not to notice my shame. I clenched a glass. It was full. I willed it up to my mouth and drank. Another one was put into my hand.

A man I didn't know had stolen my virginity: a short, ugly, frog-faced man. It wasn't my beautiful Billy, or even gentle Ken. My dreams had been sucked into a void.

When the pub closed, I forced my legs out the door.

A bloke called Phil walked me home. 'I'll look after you,' he said as we stopped at his room.

He was nice, Phil. Why not? I thought. What does it matter now? And at least I wouldn't be alone.

12

Drinking helped. It clouded my brain and provided a beer jacket, as my mother might have called it, for my heart. Below my waist didn't have anything to do with me any more: it stayed numb. In that next week, I drank whenever I could. At work I sat in a dark little cubbyhole in a hangover haze recording numbers and counting papers. At the pub, I laughed loudly, had a cigarette glued to my fingers, made a new friend every night, and woke up in a different bed every morning, racing to my room to dress and invariably missing my bus.

At the end of the week I had to go back to Coolamon to pack up my room in preparation for my parents' move to Huskisson. Our thousand-acre farm was too small to weather the ups and downs of the climate and the market. It had needed to grow or be let go for quite a few years but nothing was able to change while Pa was still alive. When he died, right in the middle of my Higher School Certificate, there was nothing holding Dad back any more, and it wasn't long before he'd found his dream job, the secretary-manager of a bowling club on the south coast. The location didn't come as a surprise: he'd been going on fishing trips with a mate to the coast for a few years, always coming home filled with cheer and an esky full of fish and prawns.

Our house had been sold and the farm clearance sale was scheduled for the weekend. Soon, Mama would be the only one left in Coolamon.

On Friday, straight after work, my Wagga High friend Janet and I hitched a ride with one of the Marrar boys. His band was playing for a dance that night at the Marrar Hall, just nine miles short of Coolamon.

'How will you get to Coolamon from here?' Brian asked when we pulled into the main street.

'We'll be fine,' we replied. 'Thanks for the lift. We might come to the dance for a while. It'll be fun.'

I didn't want to go home to my parents, where I'd have to pretend that nothing had changed. I wanted to get drunk. I wanted to have some fun.

I saw Billy's black curly hair as soon as I walked into the dance. I wanted to grab it in my fingers but he was out of bounds and only our eyes could touch. I was aware of his presence all night and I showed off: flashing my cigarettes around, drinking, and flirting with all the farmers' sons who'd never noticed me before. See, Billy, I'm not a good girl any more. I can be a bad girl too.

It was two o'clock in the morning when we were finally dropped off outside the house in Mimosa Street. The front light was on and Dad was on the veranda in his shortie pyjamas, a cigarette dangling from his fingers.

'Is that you Dianne?' he bellowed. 'Or is it the police coming to tell us to scrape you off the road? Get in here. Get inside and see your mother.'

In the bed, my mother was colourless. She held the sheet up to her chin and didn't say anything. She just looked at me with her ghastly tear-filled eyes then slowly looked away. I wonder what she saw.

My thumping guilt kept me awake for what was left of the night. I couldn't believe that I'd been so careless. There were telephones in Marrar – it wasn't that small. The thought of calling my parents to let them know we were staying at the dance hadn't even crossed my mind – or had it? Maybe I'd just told myself it was blind oversight when actually I'd chosen not to ring because my parents might have made me go straight home. I felt chastened, wanting to blame someone else, but there was only me. I dreaded the morning, when I expected all hell to break loose.

But it didn't. Instead, my last hours in my childhood home passed in silence. My parents didn't take me to the clearance sale: I had to stay and take apart my bedroom, packing my things into boxes so a truck could take them to a strange room in a strange house in a strange town. I sat on the floor sorting my books, feeling sick. Instead of showing my parents how grown-up and responsible I was, I had merely demonstrated that I still couldn't be trusted, that I was as irresponsible as they'd always thought.

A week later, my home was gone.

I imagined that I would visit my parents occasionally in their new place but that I'd always go back to Mama and Coolamon. I hadn't reckoned on my parents' expectations: that my home was wherever they were and I would spend all my spare time with them. It would start that Christmas, barely a week after they'd moved.

My mother had arranged for Aunty Elsie and Uncle Michael to drive me to Batemans Bay, where she would meet us. When they came to pick me up from the hostel in the early afternoon of the last working day before Christmas, I wasn't there: I was at the pub. They waited for almost an hour before I finally dragged myself up the road, pretending that my watch had stopped. I promptly fell asleep in the back seat, reeking alcohol over my cousins, until I was delivered, two hours later, to my mother.

'You're a disgrace Dianne. A disgrace. You should be ashamed of yourself.'

I was, but I wasn't going to let her know that.

My parents were renting a small two-bedroom holiday flat with no yard and no chooks, in a small town that was full of retired people from Sydney. It was on a bay, so there wasn't even a proper beach. All the rules my mother had fought hard for in Coolamon had fallen off the removalist truck as it crossed the Great Dividing Range and Dad stayed long hours at the club, citing his job as an excuse. My brother, who also liked to drink, was often there too.

So it was just Mum and me that first evening, and after my mother had slammed down the plate of prawns Dad had specially organised for me, she took her hostile silence to bed. My homecoming was not turning out to be the welcome relief she'd probably hoped for.

After my dinner, I sat on the front veranda, noticing how salt took up the space of dust in the air, and lit a cigarette.

'What are you doing?' my mother demanded, no longer ensconced in her bed three rooms back but looming in the doorway.

I took a deep breath. 'Having a cigarette,' I bravely replied.

'Well, THROW IT AWAY!' she exploded, her voice ferocious with indignation and disgust. 'It's a filthy habit. You're just like your father. Don't think you can come home and do whatever you like now, missy. I won't stand for it. You make me sick. Who do you think you are? I said, THROW IT AWAY!'

'I have THROWN IT AWAY,' I snapped back, raising my voice, my foot tapping madly in the air.

'Just you wait until your father gets home. We'll see what he's got to say about this.'

Dad came home buoyed up with beer and the holiday spirit. 'What did Dianne have for dinner?' he asked, searching for gleeful gratitude.

'Prawns...and a cigarette,' spat Mum.

'What? A cigarette? Well, she can smoke wherever she likes but she can't smoke at home.'

'Ross!' This was not the reply my mother wanted to hear and she stormed back to her bed.

Tension rippled through the following days as we settled into our meagre family arrangement. I was stuck in my mother's company, where I couldn't drink, couldn't smoke and certainly couldn't talk about anything. When I was alone, panic clogged my throat so I stayed in the flat with her, sleeping as much as I could and trying not to annoy her any further. As the days passed, it wasn't just my mother that I was worried about: my period didn't come and I was terrified that I was pregnant.

After Christmas, Marg and Janet came to stay. As well as providing a buffer between my mother and me, their visit gave me a reason to leave the flat. Every night, we went off to the fair in the local park, where I felt right at home: the glaring lights and shrill cacophony of shrieks reflected the tumult in my body. The whirling and jerking of the cha-cha were also familiar to me. The flirting ride attendant spun us harder and faster each time and my head snapped back on its neck threatening to sever the connection. Adrenalin and terror rampaged from my stomach to my chest to my brain.

'This is not going to end well,' a little voice whimpered. 'It's all going to come apart and I'll sail over the trees into the water, and end up dead. Nothing can be done about it.'

I thought I was going to die, too, when I startled awake one night gasping for breath. It was like someone was sitting on my chest and I panicked. Maybe it was just from the exhaustion of trying so hard to appear normal and still being the daughter who disgusted her mother so much.

After the New Year, I scarpered back to Canberra with a new resolution on board: I was going to take the time to think things through. When my period finally came, I resolved that I wouldn't have sex again either. All good intentions, but by the time the college year started in March, I was once again binge drinking every night and losing myself in sordid sexual encounters with men I hardly knew. Every day, I determined that I wouldn't do it again but I couldn't stop myself. I had to go out so the voices didn't get me. I was desperate for people to like me and I didn't want to be the girl my mother wanted me to be. I couldn't be prim and demure: I was always going to fail at that.

When I fell in love with a surfer-haired electrician, a calm settled briefly. We met after work most days in the Monaro Mall, and the tantalising aroma of warm cinnamon from the fresh doughnut stand became the smell-track to our affair. After a few weeks, he told me that he was married, and that his wife was pregnant. By that stage, the magnetic north of my moral compass had been battered and corrupted: I'd had to walk away from Billy when I learned he had a baby coming but I couldn't walk away again.

Maybe, I thought, maybe this time he'll choose me instead of his pregnant wife.

I was wrong, of course, and not only did he not choose me but when he dropped in one day and I was out, he tried to get Carolyn to have sex with him. Another bolt in my cha-cha ride came loose.

By this time, I was living in a flat in Campbell with Janet, Carolyn, and her boyfriend. Macquarie Hostel had kicked me out for having a man in my room and Carolyn had left in solidarity. They actually thought it was Carolyn that they'd kicked out. Her boyfriend stayed a lot, but had always managed to evade the A-block security. But it was me with the man in our room when they knocked.

'We know you've got somebody in there, so open up. Come on. Open the door this instant.'

Surprisingly, I wasn't having sex with him, just offering him a shoulder to cry on because he'd had a fight with his girlfriend. When I opened the door, he tried to hide behind a chair, but they found him.

'Tomorrow you better find another place to live,' the woman snapped at me as she marched him out the door. 'We can't have this sort of carry-on here.'

The only other time I'd had a man in that room, it wasn't something I'd chosen. A bloke had invited me to dinner at the fancy restaurant on top of Red Hill. I'd felt so happy as I put on my long dark-blue evening dress with the spaghetti straps: I was going on a date.

This is what it's supposed to be like, I thought, thrilled. The man asks me out for dinner and we sip wine and talk and he asks me out again, and then again, and eventually we get married.

It all went according to my script until he brought me home and forced himself into my room, into my bed and into me. It all happened very quietly because Carolyn was asleep in her bed and I was too embarrassed to wake her up. I might have had sex with a lot of different blokes but I had to be attracted to them. I hadn't wanted to do it with this fellow even if he had bought me dinner.

I hadn't wanted to have sex with Carolyn's boyfriend's housemate either. The first night out of the hostel, we'd stayed at her boyfriend's house in Kingston. I was asleep on the sofa when I was woken by one of his housemates climbing on top of me. I hadn't even met this fellow and I didn't know what I'd done that he would think I wanted to have sex with him. I squirmed and struggled, gripping my thighs together tightly. I didn't want to make a scene. I was too ashamed.

'Stupid cunt,' he said as he finally gave up and rolled off to his own bed.

The first thing Carolyn, Janet and I did when we moved into our new flat together was to visit the doctor at the local shops. It was just brazen luck that I hadn't yet fallen pregnant. One after the other, we asked to be put on the Pill. Carolyn went in first with her boyfriend, and they were so obviously dewy-eyed in love that the doctor was very understanding. He was stern with Janet but she lied well about a long-term boyfriend who lived in Wagga. I went in last and couldn't tell a story to save my life. Still, I was self-righteously outraged when he gave me a talk about promiscuity.

'Who does he think he is?'

The visit to the doctor was in time for Janet and me, but too late for Carolyn. Within a couple of months, she was married and living in the suburbs, her university study put on hold.

The Pill took away the daily stress of getting pregnant but it also meant that there was no longer any excuse to not have sex; not that the lack of contraception had seemed to bother anyone but me. It was the 1970s and everybody was doing it, weren't they? Janet and I shared a bedroom with twin single beds and even that didn't stop us bringing men home. They never stayed the night, though: that way, you could all pretend it hadn't really happened.

13

Les was the first fellow to stay the night. He was also the first bloke I could introduce to my parents, and I was planning to do that in the summer, when he would be holidaying with his family near Huskisson.

We met at a dance at the ANU. I was standing on the edge of a group while Janet wooed the lion-maned Clayton. I was ill at ease among the university and School of Art students pulsing around me, an interloper from the Canberra College of Advanced Education, which had no history in its walls, no graffiti in the toilets, and far too many public servants who dropped in for a tutorial and then disappeared. I might have been doing a Bachelor of Arts but everybody knew it wouldn't have the same status as an ANU BA, and besides, it was in librarianship.

'Hello,' a voice shouted through the music, and I turned to see a bloke with golden hair falling to his shoulders, a lopsided smile and a square jaw, grinning down at me.

'You're a friend of Janet's, aren't you?'

He sounded posh, like he'd been to a private school, but it turned out he was just a Canberra boy who'd gone to Telopea High. Most of the kids I'd met who'd grown up in Canberra sounded like that – up themselves, as we used to say in Coolamon. Their fathers wore ties to work and it was dandruff dusting their jackets, not paddock dirt. These kids never had to trail sticks around dusty roads waiting for the time to pass, and their parents had probably given them pocket money. They seemed more confident than us country kids, and acted like they could have whatever they wanted. One girl came to stay at our flat for a weekend and the next time I saw her at college she was wearing Janet's clothes.

'Isn't that Janet's top?' I'd asked hesitantly.

'What? This? No, I've had it for ages.'

We never invited her again.

'Janet says you live in Campbell,' Les shouted above the music. 'Small world,' he laughed. 'I live in Campbell too.'

I knew by then that parts of Campbell were very posh. When I'd visited the house of a girl who was doing librarianship with me, I'd climbed a sweep of stairs to her front door and when I looked behind me, I could see over the city. That's pretty grand, I thought. They must have a lot of money. I should have worn better clothes.

The only other family home I'd visited in Canberra belonged to rich people too. It was in Red Hill, and it didn't look over the city but it had a tennis court in the backyard and an immaculate front lawn that swept from the paved porch down to the gutter. I wasn't sure if you could even walk on it, but I reckoned there wouldn't be any bindi-eyes if you did.

The mother of that house had sniffed her nose up at me when she opened the door to my hesitant knock. We'd already met, sort of, when I'd rung to talk to Janet who was staying there with her old boarding school friend.

'Hello,' I'd said timidly when a very plummy voice had answered the phone. 'Could I speak to Janet, please?'

She told Janet I was very rude. Apparently, I should have said something different.

I wondered if Les's house could see the city, or if it had a tennis court.

The next night, we met at the bar again, sitting awkwardly next to each other while Janet and Clayton continued their flirting fest.

'I'm getting tired,' yawned Les eventually. 'What about you? I haven't got a car, but I could walk you home.'

It was a frosty August night and our breaths were visible as we walked from the ANU through the deserted city centre. We passed the Blue Moon café where Aunty Marie had her wartime wedding reception and the elastic on my mother's underpants had snapped and she'd had to step out of them so Grandmother Whitby could scoop them up and stuff them in her handbag. We walked along the dark streets of Reid, where my mother had once boarded, and across Anzac Parade. At one end hovered the War Memorial, where Paul had slammed his finger in the door of Uncle John's ute when we were kids. At the other end, on the far side of the lake, Parliament House gleamed against the black sky.

'My father works there,' said Les.

'Really? So does my uncle. And my grandfather used to as well. Fancy that.'

We talked all the way home. It was the best foreplay I'd ever had.

We talked about our studies…

'I'm doing economics,' he said. 'I don't know if I can stick at it. It's just a load of capitalist propaganda really.'

…about Coolamon…

'God, that must have been stifling.'

We discovered we both had fathers who liked to drink and mothers who didn't, but our worlds really meshed when we worked out that he'd played tennis against my cousin Gloria.

'Bloody hell,' I'd exclaimed, 'we're almost related!'

We crammed together in my single bed, still shivering from the icy walk.

'This is what the Eskimos do to get warm,' Les told me. 'They take off their clothes and huddle together.'

That's different, I noted silently, a bloke taking all his clothes off.

And he continued to astound me. 'Are you okay?' he asked when we were having sex.

'Mmm, uh huh,' I murmured. What was I supposed to say? Below my waist still felt dead but my arms and legs were melting into syrup.

'Did you come?' he asked.

I didn't know what he meant, and again, what was I supposed to say?

'Mmm hmm.'

I knew from Janet that something was supposed to happen to make sex feel good but I didn't know what it was, or whether I'd felt it.

When I woke up the next morning and Les was still in my bed, I smiled secretly and crossed my fingers. Maybe he'll be the one who'll want to stay around.

And he was. Within a week, we were a couple and the walk from the uni to Campbell became our regular route. We'd take it in turns to guide the other one home with their eyes shut, occasionally letting each other trip down a gutter, but always holding on tight, laughing.

Within three weeks, I'd told him that I loved him.

Being in love with Les was almost as painful as it had been with Billy. When I was with him, I couldn't get enough of him and I sulked if he was distracted. When I wasn't with him, I felt aimless, only half alive. Our first year together was marked by my tearstains. I cried at the drop of a hat, sensitive to every nuance of meaning and look.

'You look nice today' meant I looked horrible yesterday.

'That's an interesting thing you've done with your hair' meant he hated it.

When our first argument erupted in the lounge room of the flat, I thought I would die. I flung myself downstairs, threw myself onto the bed, and wept loudly into my pillow, trying to drown out the voices in my head. 'He's going to leave you. You're always going to be alone.'

I sobbed until my throat ached and I had to snatch for breath. There seemed no way back from the desolation. Life might as well be over. I remembered the bottle of valium the Coolamon doctor had prescribed for my period pain. I hadn't needed to take any since I started taking the Pill, so the bottle was still almost full.

I stumbled to the bathroom and found it tucked at the back of a cabinet shelf. I fumbled with the cap until it came free then poured the contents into my shaking hand, tears blinding me as they trickled out.

This will stop the pain, I thought. I just want to make it go away.

Spasms of anguish doubled me over and, with one jerking sob, every tiny pill jumped, slid or cartwheeled out of my hand and into the basin.

The shock of being thwarted stilled my sobs. I scrabbled to retrieve them but I could hardly see through my swollen, blurry eyes and as I tried to scoop them up they disintegrated, sodden from the tears drenching the porcelain and the watery scum around the plughole.

I'm just useless, I thought. I can't even kill myself right.

I slunk back to my bed and burrowed into its darkness.

After a while, Les came down the stairs and squashed onto the bed next to me. I moved slightly to give him more room but not so he might notice.

'Do you want me to go home?' he asked.

'No,' I sniffled.

'Do you want a cup of tea?'

'No.'

'Okay. Move over then.'

By morning, we had made up.

A lot of the time, I didn't even know why I was crying. My moods were like a swing in the wind. I was jealous of everyone and everything, and Les didn't help.

'I'm going to love you forever,' he told me one day.

'I think I'd like to date other girls as well,' he said another day.

There was an ex-girlfriend who I was particularly jealous of, a Canberra girl. They'd been teenage sweethearts and she threw her arms around him whenever she saw him, ignoring me completely. I stewed in fear that maybe she'd felt about Les how I'd felt about Billy, that maybe she still dreamed about him like I dreamed about Billy: intense, teasing dreams. Maybe she wanted Les back; maybe, because she'd grown up in Canberra, she'd assume she could have him.

I was jealous, too, knowing that they'd driven around together in his little red sports car. I tortured myself picturing it: their straight, white teeth flashing as they laughed, the warm wind making their long hair dance, envious people turning to watch the beautiful young couple in such a romantic car. This was the car I only ever saw sitting on the nature strip outside his parents' house, the grass curling up its sides.

'It just needs a bit of work,' he said. 'When I've got the money, I'll get it fixed.'

His father wanted to mow the nature strip before that happened and Les had to get rid of it. It was still to be buses or, as my mother said, Shanks's pony, for me.

Having a steady and respectable boyfriend took me a step further out of my mother's reach, or so I hoped. I thought she'd no longer terrify me and that there'd be no more barbs to shoot into my skin. But when she and Dad turned up at the flat one night a month or so into our relationship, it was obvious I'd miscalculated.

It wasn't that I wasn't expecting them but I was sure it was the next day. I hadn't been planning for them to meet Les yet, so he and Clayton were going to make themselves scarce in the morning and I'd have time to clean up the flat before they arrived in the afternoon. It certainly needed it: Janet's clothes, clean and dirty, were always a jumbled mess on the bedroom floor, along with coffee cups and food scraps, and the washing-up was only ever done when there were no cups and plates left, often by me because I caved in first. It was better than crying about it, which I'd also been known to do.

When we arrived home from the bar in Clayton's old VW the night before they were due, my stomach plummeted through the floor as I recognised my parents fogging up their car windows.

'Oh my God, it's them,' I groaned. 'They're not supposed to be here until tomorrow.'

'Well, this is a fine state of affairs, isn't it?' growled Dad as he heaved himself out of the car. 'Where have you been for God's sake? Don't you keep normal hours now you're away from home?'

'I'm really sorry,' I babbled, hoping he couldn't smell the alcohol. 'We've been at the library. Weren't you coming tomorrow?'

'You wouldn't know what day of the week it is, Dianne,' retorted Mum. 'I clearly told you it was Wednesday. And we've been here, waiting, since three o'clock. In the end, we went and had dinner with Harold and May. And we've still had to wait. I can't believe how thoughtless you are. I don't know what's going to become of you, I really don't.' She shook her head wearily.

'Hello, Janet,' she grudged. 'How do you live with her? You wouldn't do this to your parents, I'm sure. And who are these two?'

'Mum, Dad,' I said breathlessly, 'this is Les, and this is Clayton. Why don't we go up and have a cup of tea?'

Les and Clayton didn't stay very long.

There was no opportunity to empty the overflowing ashtray on my bedside table or to scoop up the sheet of contraceptive pills lying on the bed where my mother was going to sleep. Her lip had curled with disdain as we passed the open door.

'Don't bother cleaning it up now,' she sniffed. 'You must think I'm stupid, but I can see and smell what you get up to. You're a disgrace. I don't know what your grandmother would say if she could see how you live. She'd be disgusted.'

My stomach cringed with the same childhood dread and I waited for the sting of her lash once again.

'You're going to get yourself into trouble one day, miss, there's no two ways about it. You are obviously content to ruin your life, to live in a pigsty. Well, we won't be coming to stay with you again. We're obviously not welcome. You disgust me.'

They never did stay with me again, except a couple of years later when I lived in Hong Kong.

14

Before I moved to Canberra, I'd dreamed about sitting in the middle of the road and saving the world, but now all I wanted to do was sit in the uni bar and save a seat for Les. One day, he sloped through the door, his hand raking through his hair, shoulders hunched, and a frown on his brow.

'I'm chucking it in,' he announced as he brooded over a beer. 'I can't stand it any more. It's just a sausage factory. They want us all to come out the other end the same as each other. I don't want to wear a suit every day. I want to do something different.'

I was taken aback. Even though I wasn't enjoying my course, and most of the time I had trouble keeping my eyes open in the stuffy lecture theatres, it never crossed my mind that you could just stop. These city kids thought they could do anything.

'What do you want to do?' I asked as my pride in having a university student boyfriend pooled in the dregs at the bottom of my glass.

'I'd like to write, actually. That's what I'd like to do.'

Firstly, though, he needed to earn some money, and the benefits of having a wage-earner boyfriend soon made up for the disappointment of losing the uni student.

When he went to work in a record shop in Petrie Plaza, my education began in earnest, lessons that would last for my whole life. We listened to Van Morrison, Nina Simone, Randy Newman, Muddy Waters, Taj Mahal and God himself, Bob Dylan: for the first time, I wasn't out of tune as I sang about motorpsycho nightmares and simple twists of fate.

Politics was on the curriculum too. The 1974 double dissolution election would be the first time I could vote and Les schooled me well, much as Mr Padovan had done. He and Les were the most radical people I'd ever met – in those days, voting Labor was pretty radical, at least in my family. I learnt about universal health care, land rights, and women's right to have an abortion. Les gave me a Vote Labor badge and I wore it proudly, even when I went into Mama's kitchen.

'Dianne, how could you?' she gasped. 'Don't you know you would have been born with a silver spoon in your mouth if your grandfather hadn't drunk the farm away? You should be voting for Malcolm Fraser.'

Aunty Mavis and her cronies at the golf club were horrified too.

'Don't be ridiculous, Dianne,' said Mavis as she ashed her cigarette. 'You don't know what you're talking about.'

'Labor! Spare us!' said another as she sipped her wine. 'They're just a bunch of commies. I don't know what your father would say if he saw you wearing that.'

Grrr, splutter, splutter, is what Dad would say, what he said whenever the subject came around to politics.

They were right, though: I didn't really know what I was talking about. Nobody had ever talked to me about Australian politics before but I trusted Les, even if I wasn't a very good pupil.

'Want to come to the public gallery at Parliament House tomorrow?' asked one of the girlfriends in our group who worked for a new member of parliament called Paul Keating. 'I've got a spare ticket.'

'Nah, thanks, but I really need to study,' I replied, certain that, on the boredom scale, it would be on a par with visiting an art gallery.

The next day, I was sitting vacantly twiddling my hair in front of daytime television when there was a newsflash. 'The Governor General has sacked the Whitlam government.'

It was 11 November 1975.

While I was a mediocre student of politics and culture, I scored low at Les's other main lesson: how to be the ideal girlfriend.

Sometimes he had to resort to sledgehammer tactics. 'Why don't you go on a diet?' he suggested more than once.

His ideal girl was thin, like him, like all his family were. He thought

I could be skinny too, if I just ate less. Curvy breasts were acceptable but curvy hips were not. I'd tried a lot of diets in my life –Twiggy was the role model for my generation – but nothing ever changed: my thighs still rubbed together, my bones were still too big, and my belly was always round.

'Maybe if you did more exercise,' he'd say.

The ideal girl was physically fit as well. I couldn't run to save my life, or vault, or balance. Now, I think it might have been because of my very splayed feet, but then I thought it had something to do with the day in primary school when I was doing a somersault and hurt my back. I'd blacked out and seen stars, and after that I'd been physically timid, afraid of hurting myself, afraid of making a fool of myself.

'God, you're hopeless, Lucas,' the girls would say when I missed an easy catch in softball.

'Look at her run,' they'd laugh as I came last with the fattest girl in the class.

On athletics days, I told my mother my back was sore and she'd write a note to the teachers saying I didn't have to do it.

That sort of shenanigans wouldn't have fooled Les. He hauled me along to play cricket with his mates, regardless of my pleading. I begged off firmly, though, after the boys asked me if my box was all right when I was batting and I, not knowing what they meant, said yes, and they laughed at me.

He took me on weekend walks in the bush too. Just the anticipation made me feel sluggish and winded but, as long as it wasn't too hot, too cold, too blowy, or too wet, and as long as my shoes didn't give me blisters, I sometimes enjoyed myself. I didn't enjoy it if I had to rock-hop across streams or scramble up steep slopes. Then, I'd end up feeling totally hopeless and lose the capacity to laugh at anything, let alone myself.

When his family invited me on a weekend snow trip, I was excited. I'd never seen the snow before. The school had organised a day trip when I was fourteen but, as much as I'd cried and raged, my parents were adamant that I couldn't go. It never crossed my mind that we mightn't have been able to afford it.

Les kitted me out with boots and a pair of skis and took me on a chairlift up the slopes. As the ground fell further and further away, I was white-knuckled. When the chair swayed with the breeze, I was sickeningly aware of the thin pieces of metal that were holding us up. We arrived at the top and I copied the family as they strapped on their skis. With one in place, I reached for the second and started sliding towards the chasm beneath the chairlift. Everyone was shouting at me and I knew I was going to die. I threw myself onto the snow horror-struck, shakily detached the one ski and crawled back up the slope where I spent the day sitting in a tree shredding leaves and generally feeling sorry for myself.

'Do you want to have another go, Di?' they kept asking.

'No, quite happy, thanks,' I'd say, too afraid to move.

Another time, Les suggested we go tobogganing. I thought that would be safe, but as we careered down the hill, I screamed with terror. It wasn't as smooth as I'd expected and before too long one of the bumps threw me off. Unfortunately, my foot was stuck and I was dragged downhill, my layers of clothing unravelling, my bare skin skidding against the snow.

'Stop!' I shouted. 'Stop! Stop!'

Les laughed and kept going.

'Fucking stop!' I screamed. The first time I'd said that word out aloud.

He took notice of me then, and I was on crutches for a week.

'Why do you even stay with me?' I wailed to him once.

'Because you're fun to be with,' he'd replied.

I didn't know what he meant. The only thing I was good at was drinking. I liked it better than anything else and, once started, I never wanted to stop. I even developed a liking for beer, especially when a middy was only twenty cents in the uni bar. With a drink in my hand, I felt like I had an extra coat on, one that held me together firmly and hid the bits I didn't want anybody to see. That was all right early in the evening but, as I became drunker, the coat started to slough off. I could still drive, even if it was hard to tell which blurry road I should follow, and I only ever had one blackout, and that was after a night drinking white wine. Well, I won't drink that again, I decided.

I wasn't a morose or a surly drunk but, when I fell asleep at a friend's house and Les woke me up to go home, I woke up swinging my fists.

Except for the white wine night, I remembered everything the next day: how raucous I'd been, the silly things I'd said, if I'd vomited, where I'd vomited. Remembering was a good thing – it meant I wasn't an alcoholic – but it was bad too. When I woke up in the morning after a night when my extra coat had fallen off, exposing my nakedness, I couldn't bear to face anybody in case they had seen into my secret corners. I'd lie in bed for hours, squeezing my eyes shut if anybody came into the room, putting off the inevitable reckoning for as long as I could.

Les liked to drink too, but he didn't want to. He aspired to an ascetic lifestyle, where his mind and body would be in peak condition, and when he drank too much or smoked too many cigarettes, he'd pound his chest in the shower punishing himself for his lapse. I liked it when he lapsed: his grin became cheesier, his bones softened, and he loved me more.

We'd been together a couple of years when the invitations to engagement parties and weddings started arriving.

'You'll be next,' my friends said to me.

'No, I don't think so,' I'd smile, hiding my embarrassment.

I hoped I would, though. Marriage had been the carrot that was dangled in front of our girlish noses: it was the only future our mothers talked about. 'One day, when you've got a husband of your own…'

Helen and I had always joined the gaggle of women waiting outside the church whenever anyone was married. We wanted to see what colour the bridesmaids wore and how the bride and groom scrubbed up.

'Oh, doesn't she look beautiful,' we'd breathe, gobsmacked that the girl we saw up the street behind the counter of the chemist, or the girl who we'd looked up to at school, could look like an angel.

We scrabbled around scooping up the confetti and stuffing it in our pockets, good-luck charms while we planned our own weddings.

'My bridesmaids will wear apricot.'

'You'll be my chief bridesmaid.'

'Let's marry friends and then we can live next door to each other.'

'Yeah, and then I'll have a boy and he can marry your daughter…'

We'd squeal with excitement.

In my bedroom, I'd loosen one of the sheer curtains from its tie and drape it over my head, trying to imagine the man I would marry.

It became clear that it wasn't going to be Les.

'It's just a load of old-fashioned crap,' he pronounced. 'We don't need the sanction of the state to live together, or a piece of paper to make us legitimate. It doesn't stop people being unfaithful. Look at how many end up in divorce. We don't need to get married.'

'What about kids?' I asked, perplexed. 'Don't you want to have kids?'

'No, what's the point? There're too many people in the world already.'

Bang! Crash! That was the sound of a very large expectation hitting the floor.

The more I thought about it, I realised Les was right. We'd been living together, off and on, since he'd moved out of home. The sky hadn't caved in. But I had always kept it a secret from my parents.

'No daughter of mine will live in sin,' my mother had always said. 'That would be the last straw.'

Marriage didn't seem to have made her happy, though. Even her wedding day had been fraught: the bridesmaid's shoes didn't arrive on the plane and a new pair had to be conjured up in the few hours of the country-town shops being open on a Saturday morning; Mama's dress travelled part of the way on the untarred road to Wagga on the roof of the car; Uncle Frank, Dad's best man, lost the honeymoon money; and last but not least, the chooks for the reception at the golf club, which Mama had put into the refrigerator at the club for safe keeping, went rotten because the refrigerator broke down and no one realised until it was too late.

'I should have known,' my mother used to say.

I became quite comfortable with the idea of not getting married, but I secretly hoped that, one day, Les would change his mind about not wanting children. We still went to all the weddings, which meant Les often came to Coolamon with me. He was a buffer for the awkwardness I felt there. Where my parents had been, where my whole childhood had been, there was now a strange absence. Not turning the corner into Mimosa Street and walking through our front gate, banging the screen door as I coo-eed into the house, was as if one of my limbs had been chopped off. And nobody seemed to think I would miss it. I felt illegitimate: leaving home was one thing, having no home to return to was turning out to be something quite different. Could I even call it home any more? Were the people I had known all my life really looking at me coldly? Was I an interloper?

'What's she doing here? She doesn't belong here any more.'

I didn't feel awkward with Billy. Whenever I arrived in town, he would turn up, testament to either his well-oiled network or his second sense. Les being there didn't deter him at all.

'G'day,' he'd say, flashing me one of his beautiful smiles as he pulled up in his car, one arm hanging out the car door, the other perched on the steering wheel.

'Hi, Billy. How're you going?'

'Pretty good. You?'

'Yeah, I'm good. This is Les. Les, Billy.'

'G'day.'

'Nice to meet you.'

All the while, Billy's eyes watched me and I'd look away hoping Les didn't notice the flush in my cheeks. Although it was impossible, I still just wanted to look into his eyes forever, and the traitor in me wished Les would disappear even for five minutes.

'See ya. Good to see ya.'

'You too. Bye.'

It was at the last of the Coolamon weddings that Les and I burst apart. After the church service, he and Helen and I shared a joint in the car, but that wasn't the reason, just a harbinger of more boundaries trampled. By the time we arrived at the reception at the golf club, Helen and I were giggling uncontrollably, and I had forgotten the groom's name.

The smoke, the grog, the food, the occasion – it was all fun. There were people I hadn't seen since I moved to Canberra. There were others who had moved away as well and we passionately debated whatever trivia was at hand so we would seem more intellectual, more worldly-wise, than we had been as teenagers. We danced too, and as the evening progressed, I noticed that Les was having quite a few dances with the bride's sister-in-law. His smile was becoming quite sloppy, and when they returned from the dance floor the last time, they sat together a bit removed from the rest of us. I put it down to the fact that neither of them was from Coolamon and our gossip meant nothing to them. I watched as she draped herself against him, apparently finding him extremely hilarious. She perched herself so I couldn't see what she was saying but I could see that she was stroking his arm. I noticed when she removed herself from him and left the table. Gone to the toilet, I presumed.

A couple of minutes later, Les stood up and, ignoring me, wended his way to the men's toilet. He didn't come back. She didn't come back either. The toilets had external doors.

As the minutes ticked past, I became increasingly agitated. My hands shook as I lit one cigarette after another. I felt cold sober, my gut heavy with dread. Conversation swirled on around me and I pretended to be listening, a smile pasted on my face.

'Don't worry,' said her husband, the bride's brother, sitting down next to me. 'We can have some fun too.' He put his arm around my chair and his fingers started stroking my bare spine.

I flinched away. I'd known him all my life, had rejected similar moves when we were on a Wagga High footy trip to Gosford. I still wasn't interested.

I sat frozen to my seat, certain that all eyes were on me. Was that pity in their eyes?

'She still can't keep a boyfriend. Poor Dianne, how stupid can she be?'

Did they know that my boyfriend, my buffer, my passport to their respect, had left me stranded while he went to fuck another woman on the golf course?

After about thirty minutes, when it was obvious that their disappearance wasn't a coincidence, my agitation changed. What if they come back now? What would I do? I didn't want to be there when – if – they did. I felt ashamed enough already. I forced myself to move and asked Helen to drive me home. As we walked out, I realised that I still had the keys to Les's car in my purse. Fuck him, I thought. See how he likes that!

I crept through Mama's front door, avoiding the well-known creaky floorboards. I decided to leave the door ajar because I didn't want her to wake up if – when – he eventually came back.

I lay rigidly awake, my heart thumping, my stomach churning. All I could think of was what people would think of me. Not him. Not her.

I heard his step on the front veranda and the door closed quietly.

The next minute, he was standing beside my bed, in my grandmother's old bedroom, smiling crookedly. 'Hello,' he slurred brazenly. 'Where'd you go? Why did you take the car keys with you?'

I rose up from under the covers and punched him in the face. His smile wobbled drunkenly but didn't fall.

'Just go to bed,' I moaned. I turned towards the window and pulled the sheet over my head, shaking violently.

15

The sniping voices were back, swinging from the lightshades, cartwheeling through the silence of my two-room granny flat in Cook. 'No wonder he left you. Who would want to be with you?'

I'd never lived alone before and I was scared of every creak and bang. I couldn't invite friends around: I didn't want their pitying looks. And who could I invite anyway? I'd neglected my own friends when I was with Les, hanging around with his friends instead. I lost them when we broke up too, as well as his family.

I dreaded the weekends most, so on Friday afternoons I armed myself with survival rations to get me through the empty hours stretching ahead: beer, Jatz biscuits, liverwurst, and a trashy novel. The two days passed in a blur.

After a couple of months of this weekend hermitage, the woman who lived in the main house ambushed me. 'You can't just stay at home all the time. You're too young. I've got a friend who needs a date for some fancy function. Do me a favour and go with him, will you?'

Con was shy but good-looking. I didn't think he'd have any problem getting a date, but I did as I was asked.

The fancy function, at the Canberra Rex Hotel, was the sixtieth anniversary of the Russian Revolution and I wore my most sophisticated gown, the long blue one with the spaghetti straps. The room was filled with men in dark suits and bow ties, and women in short cocktail frocks with expensive hairdos. I didn't know anybody, not even my date. Then Con introduced me to the deputy agricultural attaché from the Russian embassy.

'Ah, you must learn how to drink vodka,' he said. 'The Russian way. I will teach you.'

The Russian way was straight.

'Take a breath,' he said. 'Drink it down. Now breathe out. If you breathe in after you swallow, there will be fire in your throat. Good! Good! You will make an excellent Russian.'

He didn't say anything about what a few straight vodkas could do to my brain and when I saw Gough Whitlam looking over everyone's heads, I pushed my way towards him determinedly.

'Gough, I just want to say how much I admire you. You're just amazing,' I slurred.

'Thank you, thank you,' he replied, glancing at me then resuming his gaze over the top of my head. I had nothing else to say.

Billy Snedden stood on the opposite side of the room so I wove my way towards him. What was he even doing there? He hates communists, doesn't he?

'You must be very proud,' I challenged, looming into his face. 'I saw your son in the paper the other day. For cheque fraud, wasn't it?'

As he blustered, Con appeared at my elbow and steered me to the car. He dropped me home, and I never saw him again.

A couple of weeks later at work, I was idly leafing through a library journal when an ad for an acquisitions librarian at a university in Melbourne caught my eye. Maybe that's what I need to do, I thought. Something totally different. There's nothing to keep me in Canberra, and Helen's in Melbourne.

She and I rarely saw each other, except in Coolamon, but it was never long before we were ten again and giggling at the minister's bald spot. She'd visited me in Canberra once. She hadn't told me exactly when she'd arrive, though, and I came home after a night at the uni bar to find her sitting on our front steps. Les and I'd visited her too, when she lived in Sydney, and Les's cousin had taken us to a very swanky penthouse bar in Kings Cross. Helen and I'd stood on the mezzanine floor drinking cocktails and sniggering as we skimmed slices of cucumber down onto the up-themselves Sydney crowd dancing below. It would be fun to live in the same city as her, maybe even in the same house. She was the closest person I had, outside my family.

When the university library offered me an interview, all expenses paid, I rang Helen to let her know I was coming, but she didn't answer. I rang at all different times that week, trying to catch her between hospital shifts, but the phone rang out every time. I'll just go and surprise her then, I decided. And I'll stay for the weekend.

Melbourne was busy, much busier than Canberra. Cars and trucks streamed past me constantly as I walked along St Kilda Road towards the library. Small saplings were hemmed in by pavement, and tall buildings lined the footpath. The air smelt different too: exhaust smoke, diesel fumes, concrete dust, excitement.

After the interview, I caught a taxi to Helen's address, but she wasn't home. I wandered up and down the street waiting, my spontaneous boldness wearing thin as the hours ticked away. Embarrassment took its place. Once again, I was a naïve country girl in a big city where people weren't always where you expected them to be. Panic set in: Helen might show up at any moment and see how ridiculous I was. I walked away quickly, praying she wasn't around the next corner. On the way home from the airport that evening, the taxi waited as I ducked into the Cook shops to get the beer, Jatz and liverwurst.

They offered me the job. By the time my response was due, I was exhausted and my head hurt: too many hours ablaze with the exhilaration of something new, too many hours screaming as the roller coaster car flashed towards the bend where failure was guaranteed. It was the first major life-changing decision I'd had to make alone and I didn't know what to do.

I sat at my desk, my hand on the phone, wondering what I was going to say. I looked out the large picture window of my office, across the CSIRO Forestry site in Yarralumla where I'd been working ever since Les's mother, the boss's secretary, had recommended me for a librarian job eighteen months before. I hadn't even had to go for an interview.

Below me was the green oval I'd jogged around a few times when I was trying to lose weight. Through the tall shady trees behind it I could just see the tennis court where Les and I had played occasionally. Out of sight, down at the end of the street, Weston Park spread out beside Lake Burley Griffin. I smiled when I remembered the hot summer lunch hours when we library girls had gone skinny-dipping with the blokes from the resources section.

Then I thought about the heat from the concrete in the Melbourne streets, and the noise that blocked out the warbling of the birds. I thought about Helen not being home; I thought about how I didn't even know where she'd gone; I thought about how I wasn't important in her life. And I started crying. 'I can't do it,' I sobbed. 'I can't go.'

My body collapsed onto the desk with relief. I didn't have to change anything: I could stay safe. Tucked in beside the relief though, were sobs of disappointment at my lack of courage, disappointment that nothing was going to change. But I needn't have worried: I didn't have to go to Melbourne for something to happen.

Marianne, my Coolamon school friend, cajoled me into joining her and her husband on a day trip to Wyangala Dam. The heat of the morning promised a stifling day ahead and I was gazing out my back-seat window wishing I could be a bird in the clear blue sky, wheeling free and weightless in the high ruffles of air, when the radio news came on.

A young man has drowned at Coff's Harbour. The twenty-four-year-old Canberra man was brought to shore by a surfer but all efforts to revive him failed. The man, Kerin Whelan…

I screamed. Kerin was Les's best mate. He was my favourite of all of them, a special person. He looked like a man, but really, he was just a bearded boy jumping out of his skin. He revelled in hosting all-night games of Five Hundred, and his gawky wit made us laugh. I'd even laughed when he told Janet and me that he couldn't swim. I thought he was joking, that it was just people like my mother who couldn't swim. On the day he died, he was standing up to his knees in water watching his mates surf. A rip had pulled him off his feet.

Until then, it had only been old people in my life who'd died: Uncle Colin, Grandmother Whitby, and Pa and Grandfather Whitby, who'd died within three weeks of each other. There was another Colin, too, a Sydney cousin, who'd died from leukaemia when he was nine and I was a baby. I only knew him from a photo in Mum's album and the letter he'd written to her tucked in behind it. I used to stare at the photo of him on a merry-go-round horse, looking so shiningly alive, and try to fathom what death meant.

This is it, I thought when Kerin drowned, the first of my friends to die. This is what happens when you get to be a grown-up.

As soon as I arrived back in Canberra, I rang Les.

'Can I come over?' he asked

'Of course.'

Our awkwardness was muted by our shared grief and we talked quietly, sipping tea, trying to understand what life was going to mean without Kerin in it.

'I don't want to be alone tonight. Can I stay?' Les asked.

'Sure. That would be good,' I replied.

We burrowed into each other, soaking in our sadness, about Kerin, but about our break-up as well. The yearning I'd had that morning to be soaring high in the air was now a raw and painful yearning to be with Les again.

I'm going to die one day, I thought, and he's the one I want to be with until then.

He must have felt the same way because, in those quiet days leading up to the funeral, we stayed close, falling back into the familiar routine of eating, sleeping, and visiting his family together. Our friends, as heartbroken as we were, didn't raise an eyebrow when we turned up together.

'I really missed you,' said Les, on the night of the funeral. 'Can we keep doing this? Being together?'

'I'd like that,' I said, my heart soaring. I wouldn't have to buy Jatz and liverwurst any more, I wouldn't be alone, and my life was going to get back to normal.

Except it didn't.

'I'm thinking about going to Hong Kong,' Les announced casually a month or so later, so casually that he might have been telling me he was popping down to the shops for milk.

It was as if every saucepan lid I owned clattered onto the floor at the same time.

'What? For a holiday?'

'No. You know Graham, my old school friend? Well, he's working for Reuters in China, and he reckons he could help me get a job on one of the Hong Kong newspapers.'

I was stunned. I busied myself making a cup of tea to hide my confusion. I knew it was one of Les's dreams to be a writer, and I knew that when Malcolm Fraser was elected, he said he'd leave the country, but I didn't think it would actually happen. What would this mean for us? What would happen to me now?

'Wow,' I finally managed to stutter. 'That's pretty amazing. When?'

'Oh, not for a few months. I need to get some money together first.'

'Uh huh.' I had my back to him, fighting back tears. I didn't want him to go. I didn't want to be alone again. I stiffened when his arms came around me.

'There's something else,' he said.

Oh, God no, I thought. Now he wants us to break up. I held my breath.

'I was wondering if maybe you wanted to come with me? Get away from here. Just the two of us. What do you reckon?'

'What? What do you mean? How?'

'Easy,' he laughed. 'I'll have a job and I'm sure you'll be able to get a job. You don't want to work in a library all the time, do you? We'll work it out.'

'How long would we go for?' I asked, my mind flitting between the excitement that would take me away and the fear that would keep me home.

'Oh, a couple of years, maybe five, maybe forever,' he laughed. 'We could catch the Trans-Siberian Railway across Russia and ride bikes through Europe. How does that sound? I'll have enough experience by then to do some freelance writing, and we'll get you a camera and you can take the photos to go with the stories. What do you reckon?'

'Yes,' I cried, throwing my arms around his neck and squeezing tight. 'Yes, yes, yes. Of course I want to come with you.'

The idea of travelling the world trumped getting married. The bike-riding plan worried me a bit but I figured I would be really fit by then, and besides, it was downhill all the way from Russia to France, wasn't it? Aunty Gene was the only person I knew who'd gone overseas, to New Zealand on her honeymoon. Now it would be Les and me. I could hardly wait.

'We'll have to get fit and healthy first,' said Les.

This time it wasn't just going to be swimming laps, not drinking and not smoking. This time we weren't going to eat either. We were going to have the cleanest, leanest bodies, inside and out. Les consulted a naturopath, barely even heard of in those days. This one used to be an Olympic athlete so no doubt he knew what he was talking about. He agreed to supervise us on a week's fast.

For a week, we stripped away all food from our diet. Morning and night, we took turns in the bathroom, squatting over a bucket and using a long rubber hose and warm water to give ourselves an enema.

The first few days were fun.

'Your dinner, sir,' I'd say as I gave Les a glass of the warm broth from cooking vegetables.

Colours were brighter, the light became sharper, and there was so much spare time for reading and sleeping I was exhilarated.

'I might never eat again,' I crowed.

After five days, though, I didn't feel good any more: I was lethargic and emotional, and my brain was as clear as a scrambled egg. I rang Les from work. 'Please,' I sobbed, 'can I eat again? Please, say I can. I really need to eat. Please, Les. I can't do it any more.'

'It's only another two days, Di. You can do it. You'll be fine. Just two more days.'

Fasts are supposed to be broken gradually, introducing juices then raw foods before moving on to steamed vegetables and working your way up to the fish and chips. It should take at least a week. Two days after my meltdown, when we were only supposed to eat raw vegetables, Les's little brother flourished a sausage roll in front of me and I couldn't help myself: I grabbed it and scoffed it down. Nothing had ever tasted so good, even without tomato sauce. Within a week, I'd put on more than half a stone, my stomach was bloated, and I had constant indigestion.

The heartburn intensified when Les decided that he'd leave before me. He said he needed to get to Hong Kong in case an opportunity arose.

'What if I leave from Darwin?' he suggested. 'We could drive up together. Make a holiday of it. We can sell the car there and you can fly back. And then get ready to come and meet me when I get a job.'

I hadn't been to the Northern Territory before, or Queensland, or even northern New South Wales. Some of my college friends were teaching in the Territory, though, so we'd have places to stay and people to see.

'Okay, let's do it,' I agreed.

The old green Corona made it, without a hiccup. We drove non-stop through the outback never-never of Queensland, except for overnights in whatever dingy motel room was available. There was never a minibar, which suited Les, but not me. There was to be no drinking, no smoking, and hardly a word to another soul. Most evenings I sulked because I itched to sit in the pub. I could feel the locals looking at us like they thought we were up ourselves because we didn't, and they looked at Les as if he was an alien when he tried to order a vegetarian meal. Like my father, they thought that was a sin against nature.

'What rubbish!' Dad had blustered when he found out Les was going vegetarian. 'What do you think sheep and cows are for anyway?'

For strolling across roads, I could have answered. I was used to sheep wandering across the road. They moved slowly, but they moved. Not cows. We'd be driving through the thick golden haze cast by the setting sun and suddenly a bloody great cow would loom up in front of the car. Luckily, the brakes worked.

I thought about Coolamon a lot as we drove through the small country towns that got further and further apart. We had to swap the driving at least every hour. The beating-down sun and the emptiness that stretched to a wavering mirage on the horizon lulled our brains into torpor, even with Bob Dylan singing from our tinny cassette player.

When we finally saw the bright bougainvillea cascading over the steep roadsides as we drove up the Stuart Highway, we woke up, and by the time we arrived in Darwin, the week of driving was but a blur in our memories.

'You'll be needing a beer after that drive, for sure,' my college friend Steve said jovially. 'Come on, let's go to the pub.'

'Ah,' I breathed, my insides immediately relaxing, 'something I'm familiar with.'

But there was nothing familiar about a pub with steel mesh for walls, and nothing familiar about the clusters of Aboriginal people at the bottle shop window. I tried not to stare but I'd never been so close to black people before.

'Don't the Aborigines like to drink in the bar?' I asked.

'They're not allowed,' my friends answered in unison.

'It's the Australian apartheid system,' continued Annette, Steve's wife. 'They're only allowed to buy grog to take away.'

'Yeah, and then everyone complains when they drink it in the park. They can't win,' finished Steve, wiping the froth from his moustache.

That doesn't seem right, I thought, but before I could think about it any longer, Les returned to the table with a packet of cigars in his hand.

'They're not cigarettes,' he hooted, 'so we're safe.'

We smoked the whole packet between us that night, and did our best to keep up with the hard-drinking whitefella Territorians who joked a lot about going troppo. For once, it wasn't just me: we were both extremely sick.

'Welcome to Darwin,' laughed our friends.

A couple of days later, having obtained the necessary permits, we caught a small plane to Groote Eylandt, where our friend Grant was teaching. We stayed with him and his wife Toni at Angurugu, under the stern gaze of Christian missionaries who frowned upon couples holding hands, black or white. We were there when Elvis Presley died and Toni and I cried together on the lounge. We spent a lot of time at the river and the kids laughed as we fell from the rope swing. There were carvings in trees, hearts with initials, and TFBS scratched beside them.

'What's that mean?' I asked Toni.

'That's For Bloody Sure.'

After an outdoor screening of *The Count of Monte Cristo*, the kids wielded sticks for swords and leapt from the riverbank recreating the action scenes. One night, there was a community dance and the band set up on the back of a truck. Half of them played with their backs to the audience and dust rose as everyone's feet stomped. We camped at the river mouth and fished in the sea. We dug the ute out of a sand bog. We drank at the galvanised Alyangula club. We wandered around waving back to all who passed. We didn't want to leave, but we only had permission to stay for two weeks.

On our way back to Darwin, we stopped at Nhulunbuy on the Gove Peninsula to visit yet more teaching friends. After the simplicity of the Aboriginal community we'd just left, I was revolted by the plastic, glitzy, world of the white mining community. Kids brandishing plastic swords threw tantrums in the supermarket aisles. This was my culture, supposedly, and it looked tacky and shallow. I wanted to be back in the spontaneous world of the Angurugu kids, where fun was found in the natural world and babies were handed around from arm to arm. I didn't want to have a white baby if it was like a Nhulunbuy kid. I wanted a black one. TFBS.

After a camping trip to Kakadu and the East Alligator river, where the barramundi jumped and splashed in the dawn and every tyre on the car burst, I was saying goodbye to Les and winging my way back to Canberra over the most startlingly magnificent red country I'd never imagined. That dried my tears up.

In the next few months leading up to my own exodus, I flip-flopped between exhilaration, nervous excitement and loneliness. Every day, I rushed home to see if there was an airmail envelope from Les.

'Hurry up and come,' he wrote. 'I miss you, love of my life, light of my life. Get fit, don't drink too much, and just get here soon.'

I wanted to surprise Les, to arrive looking glamorous and sylphlike, but it was impossible to achieve. The last few weeks were crammed with goodbyes. I didn't know when I'd be back so I had to see everyone I'd ever known, in Coolamon and in Canberra, and that involved a lot of drinking and eating.

When the big day arrived, I decided on bohemian *savoir faire* and chose an ankle length dress in soft Indian cotton with a brown and maroon paisley design. Its billows hid the extra half stone I'd put on since saying goodbye to Les in Darwin. I slung two strands of wooden brown beads around my neck, because that's what casually elegant women did, and I was ready.

There was a party to see me off at Sydney airport: my parents, Les's parents, his sister, and my old school friends, Marg and Rhonda. At the departure gate, Dad held me tighter and for longer than usual. His eyes were watery, as if he was crying. I'd never seen him do that before and I swallowed the sobs that threatened to burst from my mouth.

'Look after yourself, Chicken,' he said. 'We'll miss you.'

'I will, Dad,' I muttered, hiding in his collar.

When I turned back to wave goodbye one last time, my throat convulsed as he buried his nose in a handkerchief. Mum was clinging onto his arm and tears were running down her cheeks but she was smiling bravely. I forced myself to smile and turn away to push through the doors before the accordion squeeze in my heart and the ache in my face disgorged a bucketload of tears. I would not cry in front of her.

16

'It's fucking freezing,' I stuttered to Les as he navigated me through the crush of people to get to the bus stop at Kaitak airport. 'I thought you were bringing me to an island paradise.'

'Where'd you get that idea?' he laughed. 'Didn't you read up on it before you came?'

'I was an acquisitions librarian, not a reference librarian, smartie. I knew I was coming to an island north of Australia so I presumed it was going to be tropical, you know, with men in safari suits mopping their brows.'

'It's because of the winds off the Gobi Desert, apparently.'

'Desert winds? Aren't they supposed to be hot? I've never been so cold.'

The weather wasn't the only shock to my system. Coolamon and Canberra had not prepared me for the bombardment of Hong Kong. I was a country girl who thought Melbourne and Sydney were too big, but at least they sprawled. In Hong Kong, there was nowhere to go: the harbour traffic, the road traffic, the jackhammers, planes, skyscrapers, all jammed together like an out of tune orchestra.

Les's hold on my arm was reassuring as he led me ducking and weaving through road works and slalomed us through the stream of humanity on the footpaths. My nose lingered at street stalls where noodles were steaming and sizzling, then recoiled from the stench rising from the soggy rubbish in the gutters. I felt like I was being led blindfold like we used to do between Civic and Campbell. Except then I knew where I was going to end up.

Les probably should have turned me round and put me on the first flight home that day, but neither of us knew that then. Instead, he'd booked us into the sumptuously colonial Repulse Bay Hotel for a honeymoon night before settling into our formal life of sin. The hotel was in the hills in the middle of the island, far away from the teeming band of streets that lined the harbour and faced north towards the even more jam-packed Kowloon that fronted the most populous and controversial nation on earth at the time, China.

It was a relief to arrive at the bottom of the stone steps that led up to the deep, shaded veranda. Inside, the ceilings were high, the wood was dark, and our room was very different from the motel rooms with peeling paint that I was used to. Voluminous curtains fell from ceiling to floor, and the bed was the biggest I'd ever seen. The room was huge too. It was a pity that I didn't have anything to toss about it. Thai Airlines had hoodwinked me into believing my dreams of luxury were about to come true when they'd upgraded me to first class and presented me with an orchid spray and a glass of champagne. Then they sent my luggage off on its own journey: one bag to Tokyo, and the other, my fluorescently orange nylon backpack, on a jostling six-week jaunt through airports of cities all over the world.

By the time Les and I were alone in our room, I was as wilted as my orchid spray and paralysed by the expectations of a passionate reunion. I didn't feel glamorous, or sexy. Later, sitting at the white-clothed dining table with the hotel's weighty silver cutlery in my hand, I was sure that everyone could see that I was just a bumbling country girl who didn't know her entrée fork from her main course fork. I hoped that, at least, nobody would notice that I would be wearing the same damp, grimy hem to every meal.

That dress had been a problem from the start and, by the time my first bag was returned to me, it was extremely shabby, with a ripped seam testimony to how unsuitable a choice it had been. It hobbled me: I couldn't stride, clear a puddle or climb easily into a bus, and it was no protection from a Gobi Desert winter. It suited me, though: it matched my inadequate preparation and portended my difficulty in shoehorning a Coolamon girl into an international metropolis.

I don't know if I could have laid the blame on Thai Airlines for losing another bag too, the one in which I'd so carefully packed my newly acquired confidence, my more grown-up self. These were the fragile legacies of Les and me breaking up and making up, of Kerin's death, and of our trip to the Top End. With Les, I'd made the decision to embark on this life-changing journey, and my backbone had seemed stronger, but it became obvious pretty quickly that I was going to find it very hard to hang onto all of it in the massive stew that was Hong Kong.

Les had rented us a flat in Shaukiwan. 'I want to live among the real people,' he said, 'not just a bunch of expats.'

I was happy with his choice, even though we were the only gweilos, white devils, around, and English was a very foreign language. Helen and I always joked that Coolamon had turned us into reverse snobs, and we often made snide comments and looked down our noses at the people who looked down theirs. Still, I was intimidated and, to be truthful, slightly envious, of the expat community who lived on the Peak: the wealthier you were, the wider and higher your view of the neon city sparkling below.

I'd been a bit worried that Les would settle us into a rat-infested shack, but instead we had a new flat on the twenty-third floor of a thirty-storey tower block at Tai Koo Shing. There were as many people in our block as there were in the Coolamon shire, about a thousand, and there were four tower blocks already with plans for fifty in total. We could watch planes come in to land and take off from the airport and we looked down into a concrete plaza where kids bounced balls under the watchful eyes of amahs and grandmothers. At six o'clock in the morning, there was a t'ai chi class in the plaza and, for a few weeks, Les and I joined in enthusiastically. The instructions were in Cantonese and we were always a step or two behind everyone else, grasping the bird's tail when we should have been repulsing the monkey. Not that anyone minded; they just kept smiling at us.

At first, I revelled in the differences. I loved being on the buses and trams even when kids in spick and span white school shirts and blazers stared at me. I swapped smiles with women wrangling their shopping and played silent peekaboo with babies strapped on their mothers' backs. I found I enjoyed the solitude in the middle of a crowd where conversations I couldn't understand swirled around. I was excited when I started recognising similarities between people here and people at home: the boy on the tram who had the same cheekbones as Les's little brother, the woman with the same sprinkling of freckles across her nose as the girl I worked with at Forestry.

I was never intimidated by the people around Shaukiwan but every day when I joined the locals in their daily visit to the vegetable markets I felt like Gulliver in Lilliput, towering over the small-boned Chinese women and men who commented to each other, I'm sure, on my large bones and ample padding. I pushed through their stares and pasted on a smile as I hesitated at each stall, trying to decipher the green cabbage from the Chinese cabbage from the mustard cabbage, gathering my courage to try out my slowly accruing smattering of Cantonese. I didn't want to be like the English woman I saw at a market one day who was complaining loudly because the stall keeper didn't speak English.

'*Gei chin ah?*' I would ask. 'How much for the beans I'm pointing at?'

'*Saam go.*'

Oh God, she's answered me in Cantonese. What did she say? Did she say three or thirty? What will I say? She's still talking to me. I'll just give her some money and she'll give me change.

'OK. *M'goi lei*. Thank you.'

Sometimes I ended up with three catties of bean sprouts for one dollar instead of one catty for thirty cents.

Les and I started Cantonese classes soon after I arrived. I was determined to become fluent in the language, where some sounds, like ng, that I didn't even have to think about in English, have their own lives, and where vocal tones can change the meaning of a word. The pattern of tones was like a piano scale: up from the middle to the top, the very top, down to the middle, down to the bottom, the very bottom, and up to the middle. It was challenging for a flat Aussie accent. When I asked for a lemonade, I could be telling the waiter that his fly was undone, but on the minibuses I must have been speaking a whole different dialect.

'*Tai Koo Shing ahhh,*' I would call as my stop was coming up.

'Huh?' The driver would stare at me in the rear-view mirror.

'*Tai Koo Shing aahh, m'goi lei.*'

'Huh?'

The ten other passengers would just stare at me as the bus whizzed past my stop and I would have to crawl out ignominiously behind the next person alighting. How many ways were there to say it?

I was still tone-deaf months later when, in a little shop in the seaside village of Shek O, I asked for six bottles of beer. Everyone in the shop burst out laughing.

Mortified, I waited for my language-fluent Vietnamese friend to stop rolling around the floor and explain.

'You asked for six pieces of penis,' he guffawed, heading off into another great peal of mirth.

Try as I might, the Cantonese I was learning was not helping me to blend in. It didn't help me in photography class either. Les had kept his promise and bought me a brand-new Nikon SLR, a far more sophisticated camera than my eight-shilling plastic Snappy camera from the Coles Variety shop in Wagga. I didn't even know what SLR meant and I didn't find out in class. I didn't learn anything about F-stops and apertures either, just that when I looked through the viewfinder my camera had a system of little red lights and I should twiddle the knob until the red light was on the middle setting.

I was hesitant about carrying my camera around Shaukiwan: there was already enough attention on me, and it wasn't just my size and hair colour that stood me apart. The locals all fitted neatly into their clothes, whether they were the vegetable sellers in their traditional black or blue Mao-type suits or white shirts and black slacks, or the young professional women in their frilly, pastel frocks that covered them from neck to knee. My sleeveless summer tops and lumpy figure-hugging skirts were far too casual. Reflected in their hall-of-mirror eyes, despair would engulf me and I'd skulk home, only stopping to buy a wok-fried turnip cake from the portable trolley stall on the corner. It was delicious and distracting.

Even if I could have afforded to shop in one of the upmarket gweilo shops, it wouldn't have helped: I simply lacked any sense of personal style. I did know that I didn't want to wear anything frilly or flowery – thanks all the same, Mum – and that was all that was available in the affordable local shops, if they even had anything in my size. Eventually, out of sheer desperation, I had to give in and buy a couple of synthetic pieces of froth that clung electrically to all I was trying to hide. Mum would have loved them but I felt like I was in drag.

My mother wasn't the only one who thought she knew what I should wear. When we invited our landlord and his sister to dinner, they arrived, not just with their own chairs as requested, but also with an armful of presents, a Chinese tradition that has landed many a public figure in trouble. The tin of biscuits was acceptable, but I felt almost violated when these two strangers presented me with a skirt and blouse. It felt a bit too intimate even in this city where the ideas of personal space and your one-acre block was from another planet altogether.

A complete stranger at the health club, where Les had signed us up, thought she knew too. She didn't try to hide her stares while I was damaging my lower back with sit-ups, and I felt almost naked under her gaze as I sweated in the sauna.

Finally, at the dressing room mirror, as she applied her face paint, an artifice I had long since abandoned, she tossed her glossy, thick, straight, black hair in my direction. 'Can I ask you a personal question?'

'What?' I asked, taken aback.

'Do you do your hair yourself?'

'Mmm, yes,' I stuttered.

'Why don't you go to a beauty salon? It would be better if you did.'

I wanted to flush myself down the plughole but I just grabbed my gear and fled, my dignity and self-esteem trailing on the floor behind me.

Les didn't hold back either. He came home one evening with a big smile on his face. 'I thought we might go out tonight,' he announced.

'Oh, yes, please,' I gushed, throwing my arms around his neck.

He was quite happy having just his job and me, but he worked long hours, six days a week. We went out on Sundays, before he went to work, joining the family groups at a yum cha palace. While they all chattered around us, I indulged myself on the prawn dumplings, chicken's feet and barbecued pork buns that were wheeled on carts between the tables. When Les went off to work, I'd stand in the churning mass of the city summoning up the courage to do something, anything, but instead, I'd end up back at the flat watching television programs I couldn't understand, gorging on oily peanuts, smoking a contraband cigarette or three, and picking at my face.

On my birthday, I cried all day, aching with longing to see my friends, and even my family. Every night, my dreams were filled with home and I'd wake fretful and sad. Billy was in them too. We were always about to have sex but never did. Apart from my daily trip to the vegetable market, and an occasional health club visit, I spent most days mouldering in the flat alone. Les was coming home to a girlfriend whose vocal cords had atrophied, and whose brain was shrivelling.

Every few days, I'd resolve to throw off the inertia, to be a better person. I'll lose weight. I'll wake up early. I'll go out by myself. I'll try and be a lady instead of a gawky country girl. I'll be happy with Les. I don't need anybody else, and I'll try and have sex more often.

I might as well have been my own mother for all the notice I took of myself.

I did join the library. At least I could improve my mind. I borrowed a book about Nichiren Buddhism in Japan and forced myself to read it cover to cover. I read Jane Austen's *Persuasion* and pondered on the English class system. I borrowed all the works of Virginia Woolf, including the biography by her nephew. In a fit of enthusiasm, I decided I would write too, just like Virginia. I bought myself a satin and leather-bound journal and started my travel diary, copying Virginia's famous style: hence one's journal is full of stilted phrases in the third person leading one to feel that this, too, was out of one's reach.

When Les announced we were going out that night, I was thrilled at the prospect of meeting people I could talk to, as well as having some drinks and smokes. We'd been living a frugal life in the middle of one of the most exotic cities in the world, not just because of Les's ascetic desires, but because we only had a local journalist's wage coming in. I had to find a job that couldn't be filled by a local, and it was proving difficult. We were on a strict budget and every purchase was recorded in Les's little black book, even the ice creams after a Saturday excursion to Lantau or Cheung Chau. I put added strain on the budget because I couldn't bargain. It was expected even when I was buying vegetables and it was only a matter of a few cents. When it was for something bigger, like a table for the flat, my stress levels rose correspondingly and, in my fluster, I'd agree to whatever they asked.

'You paid what?' Les cried in disbelief when I told him what I'd paid for the table.

'Well, don't get me do it then,' I said. 'You know I'm hopeless.'

I hadn't yet found any clothes I could bargain for and I spent ages trying on various combinations from the ones in my cupboard to wear out with Les that night. I really wanted to go but was becoming more stressed with every change. In desperation I settled for a black shapeless dress that hid my curves and bumps. I draped my favourite black and red silk scarf around my neck and emerged ready to go.

Les looked up from the paper he was reading and shook his head. 'Yuk,' he said. 'I'm not going out with you looking like that.'

Sobs burnt my throat as I changed back into the denim skirt I wore most days. The lure of a night out overrode my desire to hide under the pillow.

17

Les needs a different girlfriend, I grumbled to myself on a daily basis. A nice Chinese girlfriend. She'll be skinny enough for him, and she won't want to smoke or drink.

Then, as he became more confident in his job as a subeditor on an English language daily, the tension that had been clouding him disappeared and his smile resurfaced. He even told me I looked nice occasionally and it felt like I had my boyfriend back. His stress and my depression had not helped our sexual relationship either. It had become a bit tedious for me: I didn't know how to make it better for him and I still wasn't sure what would make it feel better for me. Now, with the new spring in his step, Les wanted to have sex in the kitchen as well as in the bedroom, and if he was happy…

'Wait until I finish the washing up,' I laughed.

'No, I love to see a woman with her hands in the sink,' he said, nuzzling my neck and rubbing himself against me.

He took me to Wanchai one night, the red-light district of the island often frequented by sailors from around the world, and finally I saw the edgy, exotic world I craved, a million miles away from the monoculture of Coolamon, and the gangliness of Canberra. When we left the colourful streets and headed down to the more industrial waterfront, my steps became more hesitant.

'Where are we going?'

'This must be it,' he murmured.

We climbed a narrow, dark staircase to the first floor and stopped at a green door with a little shutter window in the top half.

'It looks like we've walked onto the set of Hong Kong,' I whispered. 'You know, that television show in the 60s that had Rod Taylor in it. I loved that show.'

Behind the door, though, wasn't a triad headquarters, but a small, smoky, dimly lit room with a few tables scattered in the middle and a bar along one wall. Ranged at the bar was a melting pot of journalists who, like Les, worked on the local Hong Kong newspapers, as well as some from obscure, specialist international publications, which, if you believed the movies (and I did), could have been fronts for the CIA or KGB. This was the Hong Kong Press Club, not to be confused with the Foreign Correspondents Club, where I never went but which would have been a lot posher than this seedy dive.

'So, Di, you studied literature?' asked Jack, the expat Aussie who was a legend in the Hong Kong journalists' world, his glasses falling down his nose. 'What about Australian poetry? How many Australian poems can you recite? We should be learning them, not this English stuff. Let's make a pact, Di. First one to learn the *Man From Snowy River* off by heart. Okay?'

'Okay. You're on,' I said.

'Beauty bottler!' he laughed, slapping his thigh. 'Let's have another round to celebrate.'

'Oh, you'll celebrate anything,' said Maggie, a journalist herself, as well as Jack's wife. 'Don't worry,' she said to me. 'We'll find you a job. Leave it with me. Oh, it's so lovely to have another woman to talk to, and an Aussie one as well. How do you like it here?'

By one o'clock in the morning, my heart was singing and my whole body joined in for the crescendo when I was included in the ordering of pizzas. The pizzas were delivered to the door – they didn't do that in Canberra, or anywhere in Australia that I knew – and the juicy prawns and lumps of real fish on the seafood pizza made my whole body salivate.

As we snuggled wearily on the bus going home in the early hours of the morning, I felt flushed with love for the world. I had fallen in love with Les all over again and everything was going to be all right.

It was a good time for my parents to arrive. They flew in halfway through my first year away, on a day when the temperature soared to thirty-six degrees Celsius and the humidity peaked at one hundred per cent, whatever that meant. We never had humidity in Coolamon. The air there was so dry it crackled and my hair frizzed like it was electrically charged. If there ever was any water in the air during those long hot summers, we ran outside and let it soak into our skin.

'I'm sorry we haven't got air conditioning,' I said to my mother as we came through the door.

'Don't worry,' she replied, poking her nose in our few rooms. 'It's a nice little place, Dianne, but don't you feel dizzy looking down from this high? Where are you putting us?'

'You and Dad can sleep in here,' I said, my toes curling as I pointed to the bedroom where Les and I shared the unmarried double bed. I winced, expecting a barbed reply.

'Are you sure?' was all she said. 'We don't want to turf you out. Where will you sleep?'

'Oh, we'll be right. The lounge opens up to be a mattress on the floor and we'll put it in the spare room at night.'

Was I really having this conversation with my mother? Was I really going to be sleeping in the room next to my parents on a three-quarter mattress with my boyfriend?

'Don't even think about doing anything,' I'd said to Les as we organised the room.

'This is lovely,' said Mum rubbing her hands over our plush maroon satin quilt that covered the sheets that Les and I slept on together every night, the clean sheets.

'Mmm,' I replied breathlessly, aware that the longer we were in the bedroom together the more time she had to imagine me in bed with Les and go off her rocker.

Mum and Dad were with us for about two weeks all up, with a break in the middle when they went to Taiwan for ten days. I spent most of the time with them on tenterhooks, worried what they would say or do next. I didn't want people to think that I was a tourist too. It was bad enough when they posed for photos in the rickshaws outside the Star Ferry terminal.

'Stand over here,' said Les. 'Maybe nobody will know they're with us.'

As the days passed, Mum's nostrils settled into a permanent flare and I was wriggling like an unearthed worm.

To be fair, it was her first trip overseas, and probably not the best choice for her sensibilities. It's no wonder she never roamed further than New Zealand ever again. Not only did she have to accept her daughter living in sin, but every time we left the flat, she was confronted with people who were very different to her. A lot of the time she looked like she might vomit. She was repulsed, and took deep personal offence, when Chinese men snorted the mucus up from the base of their lungs and hoicked it out in public, no matter where they were: in restaurants, on the footpaths, even out the window of double-decker buses. You never felt safe.

'Eergh! They're disgusting, and filthy,' she complained as tears welled in her eyes. 'Why don't they carry handkerchiefs? I don't know how you can live here.'

'Mum, they think it's weird that we blow our nose on a hanky and carry it around in our pocket.'

'Oh, what rot!'

She also had to put up with Dad, whose sole purpose in life was to find the next bar. As Les and I dragged them, dripping and melting, around temples resplendent with red and gold Buddhas, through an ugly concrete garden with a gaudy outcrop of gnomes, up the Peak and down the Peak, all Dad wanted to do was find the nearest gweilo bowling club.

We took them to Macau on the high-speed hydrofoil, a new experience for Les and me too. Macau was renowned for its high-rolling casinos and we'd all seen the James Bond movies where men wore tuxedos and women wore jewels and evening gowns. Mum and I had brought along our best long dresses especially. Dad wore a suit, and Les, who didn't own a suit, wore a shirt and tie. When we stepped through the doorway into the noisy gaming room, we all stopped short. We could have been walking into a railway station for the way everyone was dressed, and in front of us a young gweilo woman was sitting on the bottom stair vomiting drunkenly onto the floor.

A tall, middle-aged gweilo man brushed past us and Mum's hand darted out to grab his arm as if he could save her from falling.

'Hello,' she said breathlessly. 'Fancy running into you here. How are you?'

Dad and Les and I stared at her dumbfounded and aghast.

'Good. Good,' he mumbled as he whisked past out of her reach.

'Well, what a surprise,' she said, turning to us with a smile on her face and stars in her eyes. 'Who would have thought we'd run into him here! I just can't remember his name, though, or how I know him. What's his name, do you know?'

'Ah… Mick Young, special minister of state in the Whitlam government,' ventured Les.

And we all burst out laughing.

The laughter stopped the next afternoon. After a hot, sweaty day looking at Portuguese ruins, we were making use of the sun lounges on the hotel patio.

Dad was enjoying one of his afternoon beers in his singlet and shorts, his belly ballooning towards the sky. 'What's that place over there?' he asked, gesturing at a landmass on the near horizon.

'That's China,' replied Les. 'The Central Kingdom, they call it. On their world maps, it's always in the centre.'

'Humph!' snorted Dad.

'We're thinking about going there,' said Les. 'We can get a special permit if we live in Hong Kong and there's a train from the New Territories. Doesn't take long. It'd be an interesting place to see.'

Was he trying to be provocative or had he forgotten who he was talking to? I hardly dared breathe and pretended nothing of any import was taking place. I just kept clicking the camera shutter, taking photos of the three of them and of the far-off land mass. I could feel the tension crackling around me.

'You wouldn't be able to do that if you lived over there, Dianne,' jeered my father. 'They'd smash your camera and chuck you in jail and you'd be lucky to get out alive. You wouldn't be able to live your fancy-free lifestyle there. You both go on with a lot of rubbish. Commies, are you? Neither of you know what you're talking about. You should take a good look at yourselves and get some sense. I don't know who you think you are. Think you can just swan around doing what you like. Well, you can't…'

'Ross, Ross, that's enough. Stop it.'

Mum was agitated and pale. With the heat, Dad's drinking, now this, I was afraid she was going to collapse.

Les and I locked eyes as my parents imploded on their sun lounges and I realised how wonderful it was to have an ally during a family detonation. My brother had never been up to the task.

A few days before my parents left for home, the press club moved to new premises in the middle of Wanchai. We took them to the opening ceremony, where a feng shui priest, garbed in the lucky colour of red, swung his incense backwards and forwards, and shook his rattle to make sure everything was in correct alignment, which it was: no walls or doors had to be moved. Mum and I sat with Maggie and Ariane, another press club regular. The women were drinking wine, even though it was only lunchtime. My mother's lips tightened and she remained monosyllabic. That didn't stop Ariane who, with her posh English accent and slightly askew red lipstick, tried to win her over. With every glass of wine, her blonde bouffant slipped further from its moorage.

'Oh, he was a silly old bastard,' she slurred to my mother. 'That was my third husband, you understand. An artist, darling, but he drank. I came home one day when we were living on Samos and he was lying on the ground in front of the house. "Get up, you drunkard," I said and gave him a kick. "Get up! You're a lousy drunk," I said, "you're a disgrace," and I kicked him again. Turned out that the silly bastard wasn't drunk. He'd actually fallen from the balcony and was unconscious.' She hooted with laughter, the bouffant wobbling precariously.

'And,' she continued, ignoring Mum's lack of response, 'he'd broken his leg. How was I to know? What a mongrel. When he died, he didn't leave me anything but debts. You be careful, Di, be careful who you marry.'

I knew I wouldn't be marrying anybody, and Les and I had hardly arrived back from the airport when our relationship started teetering again. Mum and Dad had been a distracting focus. I was occupied with them every day and, when they were gone, it was just me and Les's busy work routine again. Loose ends resurfaced, and loneliness set in. This time, though, I had somewhere to go.

The new press club had none of the dark atmospheric mystery of the old place but it wasn't far from the health club where I was still trying to lose weight. Invariably, instead of doing my sit-ups, I found myself poking my nose into the club to see if there was anyone I knew. More often than not there was: Noel, another Australian journalist but, in reality, a black-haired Greek god with laughing eyes.

'Ah, fantastic, hello. Someone to talk to. How lovely. Can I get you a drink? Come on, have one with me. Tell me about yourself. How do you like Hong Kong?'

'Well, it's different to Coolamon.'

'Where?'

'Small country town. Near Wagga. Wagga Wagga.'

We laughed.

'You're a country girl! How wonderful. I always think country people are more down to earth than city dwellers. And you are, aren't you? You seem to be.'

'I don't know. I suppose so.'

'Oh, you are. You're lovely. A breath of fresh air after some of the snooty types you meet in this place. And I don't mean here at the press club.'

'What about you?' I asked. 'How long have you been here?'

'Oh, years and years. Originally from Melbourne but had to escape. Small minds. So came here, and stayed ever since. I live out in Shek O with Vincent.'

'Who's Vincent?'

'He's my lover. I'm a poof, as they say back home.'

That explained it. He was a homosexual. He wasn't looking at me with sex in his eyes, so maybe he could see me more clearly, like my friend from Forestry who I'd lived with for the few months before I'd come to join Les. He was a homosexual too, and we had a great time together. I'd even taken him to Huskisson, where our easy companionship and his lack of any male abrasiveness made my mother suspicious.

'Dianne, is your friend…um…is he…ah…is he a practising homosexual?' she whispered as I washed the dishes.

'No, Mum,' I laughed. 'He's perfected it.'

'Oh, Dianne!' she chided, flicking me with the tea towel. 'I don't know what your father will say, having one of them in his house.'

'Well, let's not tell him,' I'd suggested.

Noel and I started meeting almost daily. I always intended to have just one drink – it was the middle of the day after all – but often found myself, hours later, still drinking, still talking.

'Vincent and I aren't having such a good time at the moment,' he told me one day. 'He doesn't like my drinking, but hey, I'm an Aussie, right? What else do we do?'

'Yeah, Les doesn't like it when I drink either, especially during the day. I don't tell him now. I'm afraid I'll just never measure up and that makes me want to drink more. I feel so hopeless sometimes, like even the ones who are supposed to love me, don't.'

'And what is love anyway?' Noel asked. 'Surely, it's about loving someone just as they are. Not wanting to change them. That's why I'm here in this crazy place, as far away as I can be from home. Except my sister, she's lovely. Everyone else always wanted me to be different.'

'It feels like that for me too,' I burst out. 'Even my best friend never seemed to like me very much. I don't know, sometimes I think they're right and I'm just fucked. I'm so confused. I don't know who I am or who I'm supposed to be.'

Tears threatened to fall into my whisky and Coke and Noel put his arm around me.

'Oh, sweetheart. You're lovely just as you are. You're intelligent. I haven't had such interesting conversations with anyone else for ages. You're gorgeous. Look at your beautiful blue eyes. You're funny. People laugh when they're around you... No, don't say it. They're not laughing at you. And look how kind you are to old Uncle Lui. Other people don't care if he has to drag the bottles from the storeroom to the bar, but you always help him. You should see how his face lights up when you step out of the lift. Oh sweetie, don't be so down on yourself, and bugger them all, let's have another drink.'

We sat close, lost in thought over our drinks. I wasn't used to such intensity with a man when sex wasn't involved. Secretly, deep down, I began to wish that Noel would fall in love with me and give up men and we'd live happily ever after. It was the same old compulsive fantasy clogging my brain. Could this be the one? I knew it was betraying Les to even just think it but I couldn't stop myself. The fact didn't escape me that it probably meant I wasn't as happy with Les as I should be. I determined to try even harder.

'Why don't we do something together with Les and Vincent some time?' I suggested. 'What do you reckon?'

'Fabulous idea, Di. Let's do it. Hey, I know. I'm supposed to be going to a party on Saturday night. You could all come. Lord knows I don't want to go by myself. It'll be full of people swapping gossip and swilling champagne probably, but I should make an appearance.'

He was right: the party was crowded with beautiful people laughing and clinking glasses. It was a hot night and after standing around in a huddle surveying the room and feeling out of place, the four of us gravitated out of the hubbub to the dimly lit yard where we found a pool. I felt kissed by the universe, the luckiest girl alive to be out on such a beautiful night with these three good-looking men.

'Hey, let's have a swim,' suggested Noel.

'Did you bring your togs?' I asked. 'I wish I'd known. I love swimming.'

'No, I didn't bring mine,' answered Noel, 'but it doesn't matter, there's nobody around. We can go skinny-dipping.'

'Count me out,' said Les.

'And me,' said Vincent. 'But you two go ahead if you want to.'

So we did. Slipping into the water was as soothing as warm liquid on a sore throat. Noel and I hugged the side, smoking and chatting softly with our boyfriends in the evening quiet, occasionally giving each other a gentle splash. When I thought about his nakedness next to me, the muscles in my gut seemed to clench and relax at the same time.

'I'm going back in,' said Les. 'I need another drink and there's someone from the paper I'd really like to talk to.'

'I'll come with you,' said Vincent. 'What about you two, do you need another drink? Do you want to come in?'

'We'll follow you soon,' we chorused. 'It's so lovely in here it's hard to get out. We'll finish these drinks and have another smoke first. We won't be long. Have fun.'

We floated on our backs for a while, gazing through the trees at the starry night.

'I suppose we better go back in,' I said, lazily.

'Do you really want to?' Noel's voice was husky as he came up behind me. He trailed his fingers over my wet back.

'Mmmm, that feels good,' I managed to say before my breath gave way completely.

He pressed his body against me, nibbling my ear. I could feel his hard naked cock.

Not supposed to happen. Not supposed to happen. The words were zinging around my brain.

I turned to face him and our mouths met.

'What do you reckon?' he breathed. 'Do you want to fuck?'

'Mmm, ah, oh, okay,' I breathed in reply.

I no longer knew where I began or where I ended. My bare flesh wanted to feel nothing but his, so I let him seduce me, right there in the middle of a party, in a swimming pool with Les and Vincent not very far away. My heart thumped with pleasure and terror. The sex was short, and intense, but my limbs felt looser than they ever had and I wondered if the tremors that went through me were what other girls meant when they talked about orgasms.

It was a brief, passionate affair, but Noel remained a homosexual and I, damn it, I remained a girl.

'We better stop this,' he said as we sat in his car one afternoon.

'I know,' I agreed, sadness swelling through me.

I'd been expecting this for a couple of weeks but could never summon up the will to make the move myself.

We stopped having sex but we kept being friends, still drinking together at the press club whenever we could. Occasionally, we went out as a foursome. As I wandered home arm in arm with Les after one such night, I felt at peace with the world. The affair had matured me. Noel's attentions made me feel more solid and I was feeling more loving towards Les. I was starting a job soon, too, thanks to Maggie, who touted me to Stephen Li, a left-wing publisher of a new journal called the *China Trader*, a magazine showcasing trade opportunities between China and the English-speaking world. Stephen had hired me to be the circulation manager.

'Did you have a nice time tonight?' I asked Les, as we had a nightcap at our window watching the lights of Kowloon twinkle across the harbour.

'Yes, it was fun. I like Vincent's dry sense of humour. I'm getting used to them, you know, being together.'

'We're getting on pretty good too, aren't we? It feels like things will be okay now. I'm feeling a lot better.'

'Are you? That's good. Is that just because of the job?'

'Maybe. I don't know, I just feel more together, stronger or something.'

'You've seemed different lately. I've wondered what was going on.'

My secret had been haunting me for weeks. I didn't like not being honest with Les. It didn't seem fair that I was hiding something that had made such a difference to me.

'Well, there has been something that I want to tell you about,' I blurted. 'Noel and I had an affair.'

Les's eyes dropped.

'It didn't last long,' I babbled. 'And it ended ages ago. I don't know how it happened and I certainly didn't expect it, him being a homosexual and all.'

'Ah,' he said, staring into his drink, as if things were falling into place in his brain. 'So is that why you're feeling better?'

'A bit, I suppose. I don't know. It made me feel…it made me feel like I'm okay, or something'.

'Don't you feel like that with me?'

'I do now, but for a while I didn't.'

He looked at me.

'You always wanted me to be someone I'm not. To be thinner. To be quieter. Not to drink. Not to smoke.'

He kept looking at me, his jaw set like stone.

'It's been different lately, though. We've been having a lovely time. Haven't we?'

'I don't know,' he said, leaning back on the foam lounge. 'What are we going to do now?'

'Why do we have to do anything?' I asked. 'Why does anything have to change?'

He didn't say anything and we sat in brooding silence for what seemed like hours.

As the sun threatened to rise, I was in tears and Les had made up his mind.

'I'm sorry, Di,' he said, 'but one of us will have to go and I'm afraid that will have to be you.'

I should have been thankful he didn't punch me in the face.

18

'I can't even afford a ticket home,' I'd wailed to Ariane the day Les kicked me out. 'I'd be too embarrassed anyway. I haven't even been gone a year.'

'There, there, darling,' she'd cooed, patting my arm.

'But he doesn't want me at the flat when he gets home tonight,' I sobbed. 'What am I going to do?'

'Come and stay with me. I'll look after you.'

As I took a last look around our flat, I wished I could take the rice cooker and the beautiful Chinese quilt with me but, instead, I walked away with just the bags I'd brought with me, and the camera Les had given me. I wasn't leaving that.

I'd often wondered how Ariane spent her time when she wasn't at the club, and now I found out: she spent most of it bleary-eyed and askew, dozing over one glass of wine after the other. The odour of decay was strong, mixing with the powder and lipstick she applied to hide the evidence when she went out. Everything was on the grimy side of clean and my stomach heaved when I had to use a cup, or the bathroom. By the end of the week, all I could smell was despair, not all hers, and I was frightened.

'Come and stay with us, Di,' offered Jacqui, another press club regular.

That was the frying pan into the fire. I'd only been there a week when I was woken by an eerie whimpering and snuffling at the bedroom door. All my senses spiked with alarm. I heard Jacqui's voice shouting from the kitchen and I opened the door tentatively to find her husband, Chen, curled up in a foetal position, crying and moaning outside our door.

Jacqui clattered out of the kitchen with a knife in her hand, screaming at him. 'Call yourself a man. Stand up for yourself. You're a weakling. I can't stand the sight of you. I'll cut your balls off.'

'Jacqui, don't,' I pleaded. 'Leave him alone. You can't do this. Put it down. What about the kids?'

She looked at me blankly, walked back to the kitchen and put the knife on the bench. Then, she calmly walked to the telephone. 'My husband is having a psychotic episode and needs to go to hospital,' she said. 'Come and take him away. Hurry.'

I wasn't sure who was having the psychotic episode. It was a horror movie with Bette Davis, and I was in it. The feeling intensified when I went to meet a prospective amah the next morning to tell her the interview was off: Chen wouldn't be coming. It was early, barely seven o'clock, and there was a thick fog as I walked down the lower slopes of the Peak. The city sounds were muffled and anyone out and about was wrapped in their own cocoon. In the park, the glow of the waiting sunlight made the droplets of mist glisten, casting a golden glow over everything. An apparition in white stepped towards me, a woman dressed in a maid's white uniform. When I saw her face, I wanted to turn and run: black eyes and a red mouth sprang out from a face that was as white as her dress, a heavy-handed and badly applied layer of what could have been talcum powder. Was everybody mad?

I dragged myself back to the house that afternoon, wanting to pack my bags but with nowhere to go. Chen was home from the hospital and he and Jacqui were nuzzling and cooing at each other as they bathed their baby together. I didn't understand. Hadn't what happened the previous night been catastrophic?

I backed out the door and went to the press club.

'Have you learnt that poem yet?' cracked Jack as he bent to take his shot at pool. 'Ha ha. Got it. Your shot, Karen. Hey, Di, have you met Karen?' He indicated the woman lining up a shot. 'She's my producer, keeps me on the right bandwidth, don't ya? You two should get on like a house on fire. She's just been kicked out too. You bloody sheilas, you should behave yourselves better,' he chortled.

Before Jack had sunk the black, Karen and I had decided to find a place together. It didn't take long, and within days we'd moved into a flat on Food Street in Wan Chai. There were restaurants all around us, an Indian security guard at our door with a baseball bat, and an old-fashioned lift that jerked and shuddered when the grille clanged shut. We decided to keep it simple: there was a double mattress that we shared in one bedroom, and the other bedroom was our cupboard and ironing room.

We adopted a bent-tailed street kitten and named her Elsie Elliot, after the doyenne of the underprivileged in Hong Kong. They both poked their noses into everything. When Karen stayed out in Shek O with her ex-boyfriend, I often woke to find Ellie's furry little head on the pillow next to me, the covers pulled up around her neck, and a little paw resting lightly on my shoulder. I used to take her to the press club, where, once free of her basket, she would streak up the hessian-covered walls purring with delight. We knew she had phenomenal climbing abilities but we never could work out how she managed to skirt the outside of our building, thirteen floors up without any obvious foothold, and end up in our neighbour's bedroom.

Ellie and I adored each other – on New Year's Eve, we divvied up the fried chicken livers between us – but she was much more jealous than me. When I shared my bed with Eddie Cheng, a news photographer who looked just like Billy – tall and lean with curly black hair, and a smile that kept me warm for hours – Ellie would jump onto his back, claws extended. Eddie eventually went back to the wife I didn't know he had and, when Michael Chugani stayed, we shut the bedroom door and Ellie yowled on the other side. Michael, still wounded and uncomprehending about his wife leaving after being married for just a couple of months (after living together for seven years), introduced me to Indian politics and the dangerous Indira Gandhi as he rolled the joints. I would have stayed with him if he'd asked me, but he didn't.

I pretended to be footloose and fancy-free, like Bill Yim, a friend who was a caricaturist and cartoonist. He loved drawing lewd cartoons but he was most famous for spending a year in jail in China for subversive activities. He was a man who loved women, who ogled every woman he met but treated us as equals. I was one of the few he didn't sleep with and his friendship made me feel connected to the old city of Hong Kong, the one that tourists didn't see. Most Fridays, he led a posse of us from the press club to eat at his favourite dai-pah-dong. It was in a narrow street where we had to move our chairs aside when a car came through. The shops had closed for the day, the shutters pulled down, but lights were strung across the street and food stall woks sizzled with noodles, prawns, meats and vegetables. Stall workers rushed to make tables large enough to accommodate us and delivered Tsing Tao beers, plastic bowls and chopsticks. I was the happiest I could be as I looked around the table at the motley collection of people from all over the world that I was hanging around with. Old China hands argued and chiacked each other, and the younger ones strained to catch every word of their stories of journalistic daring.

Sometimes Les came. We couldn't avoid each other in the small local journalist community. One night, we drank too much and found ourselves sitting close, arms touching.

'It's sad it didn't work out,' we agreed as we gazed into our drinks.

'Oh, it's probably for the best,' he said. 'You look like you're having a good time.'

'Mmm, but I miss you.'

'I miss you too.'

'Maybe,' I blurted, 'if we'd had a baby, it would have been different and we'd still be together.'

For a moment he nodded. Then, when we both realised what had been said, we jumped apart. Any thoughts of falling into bed together for old times sake quickly disappeared.

'I don't know why I said that,' I confessed. 'It's not like I think about it like that.'

'Forget it. I know what you mean. But I better go. I've got an early start in the morning.'

Sometimes Bill took us to a Greek restaurant in Kowloon, where we were invited to throw our plates into the fireplace. He took us to a strip club too. This was not one of the strip clubs for the sailors in Wan Chai. Like the old press club, it was at the top of a narrow flight of stairs with a shutter in the door. Bill knocked and it slid open. When they saw it was him, the door was thrown open with a fanfare and we entered into a small low-light bar with a stage in one corner. Karen and I sat on high stools sipping gin and tonics through straws, pretending it was nothing out of the ordinary to watch what a couple of women could do with their bodies and, once, with a snake. I think it might have been a rubber one. Bill and his mates barely watched the show and in the interval Karen and I chatted to the women.

'Hi, ladies,' they chirruped. 'You like the show?'

'Yes, yes, you're great. Would you like a drink?'

'No, we don't drink but we can sit. Okay?'

'Yes, lovely, sit down.'

'Where you from?'

'Australia.'

'Ah, I would like to go to Australia. Australian men, they are big and funny, no?'

I didn't feel so alone when Karen came on these outings, the two of us on the prowl together, but she kept being drawn back into the relationship with her ex. I wanted her for myself; I wanted her style and ease in the world to rub off on me.

'I'm a feminist, Di,' she told me one day. 'You know, get rid of our bras, equality for women, that sort of thing. Women get a hard time and we've just got to get stroppy.'

That sounded pretty good to me, even though I hardly ever wore a bra anyway.

She rang me at work one Friday to say she was staying at Shek O for the weekend. 'Di, do you mind if someone stays at the flat with you for a few days? His name's Barry, and he's over from the Philippines. Just say if it's not okay.'

The Philippines. Images of being there with Noel and Vincent at New Year flashed through my mind: the heat; the colour; the police in the streets armed with machine guns. They'd taken me along as a treat, to help me get out of the depression that set in after Les kicked me out. As soon as I'd clambered into a jeepney, really just a metal shell except for the front windscreen with Mothers of Mary hanging from the rear-view mirror and prayer cards stuck in every crevice, the world seemed brighter. When the driver pushed a button on the dashboard and the Beatles filled my ears with 'Here Comes the Sun', my heart soared. 'Lucy In the Sky With Diamonds' followed and I knew I loved this country. It had offered me a glimpse of hope, and now I felt it coming close again.

When I walked through the door of my flat that evening, I was met by a scrawny, half-naked, sun-baked bloke with a flop of sun-bleached hair and a missing-toothed grin. He had a gin and tonic in one hand and a joint in the other. The sarong around his bottom half was snug.

'G'day.' he crowed. 'I'm Barry. How are ya? Would you like a gin? Here, have a toke on this.'

Before the joint was finished, we were hitting it off like old mates. We laughed a lot, although his was more of a titter really, the tip of his tongue stuck between his teeth. When he looked at me with his creased and twinkling blue eyes, it felt as if he was seeing deep inside me. Something in my chest woke up and stretched. It reminded me of how I was with Noel: aware of my depths as well as my edges. At the club that night, the bastard hustled me at pool, but I didn't mind. We flirted brazenly but the electricity between us had rushed straight past the sexual and settled on something that felt much more solid.

The next morning, I woke up vomiting and aching all over and it wasn't a hangover. I could hardly move for three days and Barry stayed with me the whole time, making cups of tea, feeding me when I could eat again, amusing me with possibly tall tales of his escape from an English aristocratic family and running away with his wife to Rhodesia, as it was, and then on to Australia. The stories became wilder after their break-up, and featured a snake in the roof to protect drugs and a cash stash, the subsequent drug bust, and then skipping the country with his girlfriend, Jen, on a thirty-foot yacht named *Pegasus*, which was now anchored in the Philippines while he did his business, whatever it was, here in Hong Kong.

When it was time for him to return to *Pegasus*, the sarong came off and he disguised the dissolute larrikin with a captain's hat, a navy-blue blazer with epaulettes, and a posh English accent. He was the epitome of the yacht captain who would be welcomed at any one of the elite yacht clubs around the world. To complete the picture, he hauled a large sailor's duffle bag over his shoulder.

'I'll give you a tip for travelling, girls,' he said. 'If you're ever carrying anything that you don't want found, always pack tall and deep, not flat and skinny.'

As he opened the door to go, he turned back to Karen and me. 'So, when are you coming?' he grinned.

'Yeah, right!' we laughed.

'I'm dead serious. When are you coming? Here's where we are. Tambobo Beach.' He passed us a scrap of paper with the details of the yacht's anchorage. 'See you girls soon.' And out the door he breezed.

I turned to Karen, my eyes gleaming. Noel and Vincent had given me a glimpse of a different life and now here was Barry offering it to me on a platter. 'Let's do it!' I yelled.

'Yes,' she laughed. 'Let's do it.'

'Woo hoo! Yahoo! We're going to the Philippines,' we sang, jiving around our tiny lounge room.

Before we went to bed that night, we'd written our resignations, sublet the flat and found a loving home for Elsie Elliot.

Karen left before me: I had to get some money together first. For six weeks, I worked at the *China Trader* office during the day and behind the bar at the press club at night. I slept in a back room at the club, too, and showered around the corner at Bill Yim's flat. With Karen gone, however, and even though I had an adventure ahead of me, the old feeling of emptiness opened up in my chest. Everyone seemed to have someone to be close to: Noel had Vincent, Les had a new girlfriend, Jack had Maggie, Jacqui had the kids and Chen, and Ariane had…well, I was scared of what Ariane had, but not scared enough to stop my own drinking. Living at the club didn't help and I came close to spinning off the planet a few times.

One of those times was when I went to a short-time hotel with a friend. These hotels were Hong Kong institutions where married couples who lived in small apartments with generations of family members could go to have sex, as well as those who weren't married and had nowhere else to do it. There was a dimly lit and richly lush one on the floor above the club and I'd been to another one where you could choose from a whole range of themed rooms. The one I went to this night was not quite so fancy but I expected it would offer some privacy. I was wrong.

We hadn't been in the room long when there was a banging on the door and three men in police uniforms burst in. I froze beneath the sheet as they loomed over us.

'Show me your passports,' demanded the man with the most stripes.

They didn't really want to see our passports. It was a ploy: they just wanted to see a black man and a white woman together.

'Get out,' yelled my friend. 'You can't just come barging in like this.'

I was shaking as I held my bit of the sheet to my chin, and sound was rushing through my ears in a jumble. Everyone seemed to be shouting.

'Show me your passport now,' the man in charge bellowed, pointing a finger at me.

'I haven't got it with me,' I stuttered. 'I live here. I don't carry it with me.'

Finally, when they'd had their eyeful, they backed their supercilious smirks out the door. I felt their contempt and I felt contemptible. I jumped out of the bed, stuffing myself into my clothes, shakily trying to sort the insides from the outsides. It was as if I was in one of my recurring nightmares, wading through thick mud and getting nowhere, running to escape a menacing figure but not moving, fumbling for door locks and not being quick enough. I was still pulling my clothes together as I fled from the lift on the ground floor and crawled underneath the security roller door to freedom. I ran through the streets, not caring what people thought.

Next morning, I jumped on the first bus to Shek O, where I threw myself into Noel's arms. 'I've never felt so disgusting,' I sobbed.

Noel held me as I wailed. 'There, there, Di,' he said as he wiped my tears. 'It'll all be okay. You'll be fine. Just put it in your memoirs under E for experience.'

*

Finally, it was the day before my plane was due to leave for the Philippines. So close, but it wasn't time to relax yet.

First, I needed to go to Central, the bustling business district, to pick up my ticket, my visa, and my money.

'Hey,' said Ron as I was about to leave the club, 'have a joint with me first.'

On the tram, people's faces started zooming in and out of focus. Their voices were amplified and the air around them seemed alive with energy. By the time we arrived in Central, I wasn't sure if I could move my body, but I put one foot after the other, and ended up on the footpath. My ears were ringing and my heart was racing. Panic surged through me when I couldn't recognise where I was. I stood stricken to the spot. Everyone is looking at me, I thought. They know I'm stoned.

Usually when I had a joint I laughed a lot and felt comfortable in my body. Now, I was an extra in a movie I knew nothing about. Sweat broke out on my face and I was terrified I might die right there, on a street corner in Central buffeted by the crushing rush of men in suits and skinny women in synthetics and high heels.

I saw a phone in front of a shop. I needed to talk to Ron. 'What's happening to me? I'm freaked out.'

'It's okay. Just relax.'

'Relax? What did you put in that joint?'

'Just a little bit of opium, Di. Enjoy it. You'll be fine.'

'Well, thanks a bloody lot,' I said and slammed down the phone.

Knowing it was only opium helped me to calm down. I'd been with people who smoked opium and they didn't die, and I wasn't losing my mind after all. I stood and breathed deeply, the tension in my body easing. The noise in my ears quietened and I recognised where I was.

I can do this, I said to myself. Just take one thing at a time.

I steered my way smoothly through the crowds like a rally car driver avoiding all obstacles. My body parts were working together perfectly and I began enjoying myself. I completed my tasks smoothly and in record time, and I made some new friends along the way: the teller who handed me my money, the young man in the airline office, and even the fellow behind the counter at the Immigration office.

'Yes,' I said to him, 'I will have a good time and, yes, I'll definitely come and see you again when I'm back in Hong Kong.'

If I ever managed to leave the place, which became doubtful the next morning when I woke up in the windowless room at the press club after just a couple of hours sleep. I lifted my head to check the clock and my stomach lurched to my mouth. My plane was due to leave in fifteen minutes. I'd fucked up again.

I sobbed with frustration as I ran to the phone in the office. Outside, it was a grey, misty morning.

'Hello, ma'am. How can I help you? Yes,' said the voice on the other end of the line, 'that plane was due to leave any minute but I'm sorry, no planes have been able to take off this morning, ma'am, because of the fog. Yes, ma'am, it will be leaving when the fog clears but it will be in a queue. I can't really say exactly when, ma'am, but not for at least another hour and a half.'

I dressed frantically, threw the last-minute things into my bag and a kiss to Ron, and raced out the door.

Please God, let there be a taxi outside, please God.

I didn't believe there was a god but he had come through for me in second year when he made Chris smile at me, and for a while he had brought Billy close. He came through for me again with a red and white taxi, its Unoccupied light shining through the fog.

My stomach churned until we crossed the harbour. The fog still hadn't lifted: I would make it to the plane.

As the plane taxied down the runway, I resolved yet again to change. This time it would be easy. I would be in the Philippines where the air was always warm, the sea was always blue, and the sun was always going to shine. I could be the person I wanted to be.

19

'Rock and Roll to Bonbonon', the sign welcomed, and the jeepney did just that as it picked its way between the potholes and gullies down the steep incline to Tambobo Beach. I clung onto the bench, trying not to pitch forward or smack my head into the roof. As we inched around a curve, and the thicket of palms lining the track thinned momentarily, I let out a gasp. I had caught a glimpse of paradise, the one from the travel magazines: a lone, white boat-shaped jewel sparkling against the blue, blue, waters of a bay. Could this really be where I was heading?

My travelling companions, a host of young men and boys, stared at me, much as they had done for the whole trip, in between murmuring to each other and laughing. When I'd hired the jeepney – with Sweetheart painted in curlicue writing above the windscreen and Praise the Lord on the rear bumper bar – they had climbed aboard for the journey to see where this strange woman with the blonde frizz was going on her own.

The first part of the journey was on the concrete paved roads heading south out of Dumaguete, the capital of Negros Oriental, one of the central Philippines Visayan islands. I sat in the open-sided sardine tin smiling as I remembered the joy I'd felt when I climbed into my first jeepney in Manila with Noel and Vincent. My smile now hid my apprehension too: would Karen and Barry be pleased to see me? Was it really all right that I was coming? I turned my face to feel the warmth rushing past and my veins pulsed to the music of the Bee Gees that was pumping out from the driver's cabin. I wanted everything to slow down, to hold this moment forever.

There were no brown paddocks stretching to the horizon, no heat-wilted clumps of sheep lying under shade trees. It wasn't Hong Kong with its spectacular high-rises. Instead, buffaloes wallowed ankle deep in waterlogged fields and cooking smoke wafted from bamboo huts that lined the road. Clothes were spread to dry on patches of grass hugging the roadside: no Hills Hoists here. Kids in faded shorts and T-shirts emblazoned with Mickey Mouse or Astro Boy carried bare-bottomed younger children who rubbed sleep out of their eyes.

Bonbonon was a tiny hamlet so far off the beaten track I started thinking that perhaps I was being abducted. A jeepney seemed to be a rare event, from the way the locals stopped and stared. Chickens squawked and flapped away from the wheels, adding to the dust that swirled around the figures with weathered faces sitting on skinny benches or standing in doorways. Pigs snuffled at the ground and more children, in similar T-shirts, waved and ran alongside. My smile was still plastered in place: what if Barry and Karen had decided to up anchor and sail away?

At the bottom of the hill, the jeepney puttered to a stop just a few metres from the water of Tambobo Bay. My eyes were hardly big enough to take it all in. Coconut palms leaned out over the narrow beach, casting a deep shade over the fifteen or so bamboo huts nestled between the hillside and the water. A couple of women in faded shifts emerged from the shade and waved shyly, tiny children peeking around their legs. Small outrigger boats had been dragged up onto the strip of sand and Karen, in her red and white bikini, was pulling a yellow dinghy up to join them.

'Di! You're here. Woo hoo,' she shouted, running towards me. She grabbed me in a big hug. 'It's so good to see you. You'll love it.'

'Coooeee,' called Barry, and there he was leaning against the railing of his boat waving his arms wide.

Even though the boat was anchored about fifty metres out, I could swear his eyes matched his skimpy bright blue Speedoes.

Phew, I thought. They are here. And they're happy to see me.

'Come on,' he called again. 'Get yourself out here. Just leave your bags. We'll get them later.'

Once it was clear that I was staying and there was nothing more to see, my Sweetheart companions waved and the jeepney chugged back up the hill towards Bonbonon and Dumaguete.

'Into the dinghy, Di,' ordered Karen. 'I'll hold it while you get in. It's a bit wet. There's a hole in it, but here's a tin for bailing it out.'

'Are you sure it'll hold two of us?'

'It'll be fine. Now, how do these bloody oars work? I haven't quite figured it out yet.'

I gripped the sides of the rowboat as Karen fumbled us out to the yacht. *Pegasus* was a lot bigger closer up and my stomach curdled when I realised that I had to get from the dinghy, which was slopping from side to side, up onto its deck.

'Isn't there a ladder?' I asked Karen.

'Not on Barry's boat. No ladder. Nothing so useful,' she laughed. 'Watch me. Watch how I do it,' and she hauled herself up using the wooden struts of the pointy stern, a feature, I was to learn, that gave *Pegasus* some distinction in the yachting world, where most yachts just had a pointy bow and a flat backside.

After weeks of practice, Karen almost flew aboard. Heaving myself on board seemed totally beyond me. I'd never climbed trees and couldn't lift my own body.

'Come on, Di, you can do it,' Barry encouraged. 'I'll give you a hand today, but never again. Okay? I'm a bloody hard captain, hey Karen?' he tittered as he stretched out his arm to steady my climb.

I bumbled and rolled my way onto the deck, bruising my ribs as I went. As I recovered, hoping I hadn't made too much of a fool of myself, I felt another pair of eyes piercing into me. I'd been so busy worrying about seeing Karen and Barry again that I'd forgotten Barry's girlfriend was on *Pegasus* as well.

'Di, this is Jen? Jen, this is Di,' offered Karen.

'Yeah, I've told her all about you,' joined in Barry,' about how you hustled me at pool and had me making you cups of tea and toast. A slave driver you were.'

'Liar! Don't believe him, Jen. He hustled me, not the other way around,' I laughed.

'Yes, I can imagine,' she said raising her eyebrows. Her thin smile didn't touch her eyes. 'Welcome aboard, Di.'

Jen was skinny, like Barry, with fair sun-bleached hair. Her nose looked like it had recently been sun-kissed but she obviously was careful with the sun because her skin was smooth and pale. Standing next to her and Karen, I felt like a whale.

'Hey, good to see you,' said Barry putting his arm around me. 'Want a joint? Jen, grab the stash, will you. Let's welcome her aboard properly. And let me show you around your new abode, my dear.'

Pegasus was a thirty-five-foot timber-hulled yacht, far superior to the modern fibreglass ones, according to Barry. Her white sides glistened in the sun, the woodwork gleamed, and her yellow deck was warmly comforting. Karen and I slept on narrow bunks below deck in the pointy end. Jen and Barry were in the bed in the main cabin that transformed into a communal lounge during the day. Below deck, there was also a galley and a head, and up above, a whole new world. Every morning when I came onto the deck, I pinched myself to make sure I wasn't dreaming, that the cloudless blue sky, tempting waters of the bay, coconut trees and nipa huts were real.

Barry was a strict captain and, while he was pretty loose about everything else in his life, he ran the boat with a strict discipline. There were rules that had to be obeyed. Everything really did have to be shipshape, in its right place. The ropes had to be coiled; the dinghy tied with the proper knot – something to do with going down a rabbit hole and then up again; and the galley had to be kept clean. Sturdy bolts secured the cupboards and drawers where our provisions and daily paraphernalia were stowed and, except for the music system that had pride of place in the cabin and a small eclectic library of books, *Pegasus* was ready to respond to the elements at a moment's notice. This could all mean the difference between survival and disaster when the boat was on the open sea. I was quite used to living with rules and Barry was far less terrifying than my mother. There was no strap in the third drawer, as far as I could see.

The first rule on *Pegasus* was that Barry was boss. The second rule was that Karen and I were there to be her crew: we were not there for a holiday. Nothing was ever done until we'd passed around a joint but Barry was a hard taskmaster with a wicked sense of humour.

'Okay, crew,' he'd say. 'Today I want you to scrape the barnacles off the hull. Here's a couple of snorkels.'

'See that rope I've rigged up over the side?' he said another day. 'I want you to give *Pegasus* a bath. Wash her down. You can hang on to the rope when you need a breather.'

We scrubbed, one-armed and dangling until my shoulders were screaming.

'Let's have a break,' suggested Karen.

'Nah, you're not getting back on deck until the job's done,' Barry snickered. 'Just hang in there.'

'But we want a smoke, Barry. Let us have a smoke break. Please.'

'You can have a smoke break. Here you go,' he grinned, leaning down and handing us a smoke each.

'At least light it for us, will you?'

'Nah,' he laughed, and handed us a box of matches as well. The glee etched on his face made his eyes even bluer.

'Bloody hell! You really are a bastard, you know. At least pass us a towel to dry our hands.'

He didn't laugh so much when Karen and Mario, a visitor from Dumaguete, sank the dinghy, losing the flippers, snorkels and a torch. Luckily, they saved his camera, and held onto the dinghy's painter – yacht-speak for the rope that ties the dinghy to the boat – so it didn't hit the bottom too. I had no idea it would be so difficult hauling a waterlogged dinghy to the surface and getting it onto the deck to dry out. Trying to turn it over when it was being held by a huge suction plug seemed almost impossible.

People have always done a double-take when I tell them that I crewed on a yacht in the Philippines. I don't know what they hear but I laugh and assure them that there was no screwing going on. Even though I'd never felt so sensual – spending each day in my bikini, my bare skin luxuriating in the warm sun and gentle breezes – I never had sex on *Pegasus*. My body was so liquidly exhausted at the end of a day's chores that I didn't give it a second thought. In fact, there was little sign of a dissolute lifestyle on board at all except at night when we lay on the deck, bleary-eyed from a fat joint, star-gazing and marvelling at the deep blue of the sky, debating if it really was the Southern Cross we could see and if so, how come? Weren't we north of the equator? And every night, as I looked up into the universe, I resolved that the next night I would take a photo of the moon behind the mast, but I never did.

During the day, Barry's demands pushed my physical limits. He delighted in not making things easy. Muscles that had resigned themselves to a lifetime of oblivion woke from their comas and, after the initial pain, stretched joyfully. He steadfastly refused to get a ladder to ease our comings and goings and he also refused to fix the machine that pulled up the anchor. Instead, Karen and I, and sometimes Jen, had to haul the slippery and barnacle-encrusted chain and rope up from the seabed, eighty feet below, by hand. Once you started, you couldn't stop because the anchor would swing and could pierce the hull. It didn't matter how puffed you were, how twisted your body was, or even if your hands bled, you just had to keep pulling. The saving grace was that we didn't have to raise the anchor very often because we didn't actually sail much. There was always a plan to go on a jaunt but something invariably came up, like the weather, or the need to careen *Pegasus* to re-paint her, or Barry had to go trucking, as he called it, dressing up in his captain's gear and heading off to Cebu or Manila for reasons only he and Jen knew.

Karen and I thought it might be for drugs, or at the least, for the clandestine smuggling of radios in this time when Marcos still gripped the country. It had to be something that was lucrative enough to keep *Pegasus* afloat: maintaining a yacht was an expensive business.

Karen and I wanted to stay afloat too. Our money wasn't going to last forever so we were always searching our brains for ways to get more.

'We could do a drug run, Barry,' suggested Karen. 'From Singapore. We could stuff it up our vaginas and it'd be easy peasy.'

'No fucking way, you two. No fucking way. Nah, you're not doing that. Over my dead body.'

There was obviously no easy money to be had and Lola, a tall skeletal matriarch of the barrio with deep brown eyes and large brown growths covering her face, confirmed that for us. She used a coconut palm frond and our cupped hands to tell our fortune. She told Jen that she would have money but it wouldn't be hers; she told Karen that she would always have a little bit of money.

'None,' she told me. 'No money for you. Look, it runs out.'

Sure enough, my cupped palm lacked a wall on one side. She also told me my first husband would be no good for me and the second would be a foreigner but he'd be all right. I would have two babies and one of them would die.

With no good news ahead of me, I felt lucky be in Tambobo. Apart from the occasional sound of a fisherman's pump-boat motor as he sought his daily catch, the laughs and shouts of children, the cackle of chooks, the crowing of roosters and the squealing of pigs, especially the ones who knew their days were numbered as the barrio's fiesta drew closer, peace wafted across the water.

There was only one English speaker in the barrio, and she also happened to have the only outlet for rum and Coke and Bowling Green cigarettes, so we got to know Florrie and her family quite well. She was heavily pregnant when I arrived but still ruled the roost. Batik, her husband, was tall and gaunt and could shinny up coconut palms with ease, his machete held in one hand. He shared the cooking and was a hands-on dad, changing nappies, rocking the little ones to sleep. When Rosalie, a serious nine-year-old, wasn't at school in Bonbonon in her best pink dress, she went with her dad on his fishing expeditions, an oversized T-shirt falling from one shoulder. Nothing much was expected of six-year-old Mary Joy, so she led a carefree existence, running between her grandmother Mumma's side and our shadows whenever we were on shore.

While Mumma's sister, Lola the fortune-teller, was tall, Mumma seemed to shrink daily. She looked after the family pig and wove together the palm fronds collected by Batik and Rosalie to fix the walls and roof of their nipa hut. She had mischievous eyes and a gummy smile.

'Black,' she said patting her head. 'White,' she said, patting her pubes. She took great delight in showing us her naked thighs and pretending to sniff Karen's fanny.

'You need a boyfriend, Mumma,' we'd laugh.

Florrie laughed at Karen and me when we turned up at the well to wash our clothes while she and the other women were doing theirs. 'No, let us do it. You don't have to do it,' she offered.

'It's okay,' I replied. 'Really. I can do my own. I'm quite used to doing it by hand.'

'No, Di. We will do it. We will make them properly clean, you will see. Don't worry.'

'I'm not worried about them getting clean, Florrie, I'm just not used to anyone doing my washing for me. It makes me feel lazy.'

'Oh, you!' She laughed at me flapping her hands in my direction. 'It's okay. You can give us a small payment.'

My whites had never been so white.

'All we want,' said the women as they sat in the cooling shade slapping and pummelling clothes with soap and rocks before spreading them in the sun, and then repeating the process, 'all we want is a washing machine.'

'No,' I cried, 'no, you don't! You'd have to have electricity and it's so lovely and quiet here. The machines are noisy, and they break down. No, don't want it. Don't change anything.'

As the words flew from my mouth, I thought of how there used to be a copper in the corner of our laundry when I was a little girl, and a laundry stick abraded silver, like driftwood. I remembered when my mother had graduated to an electric machine with a wringer, and then, the ultimate, a twin-tub that just required some pushing buttons and turning dials: you put the washing in, you took the washing out, you put the rinsing in, you took the rinsing out, and you hung it on the line. I tried to imagine my mother sitting cross-legged on a rock, her feet in the water, scrubbing Dad's shirts and pants by hand, then bathing herself and us kids at the same time as chatting to the other women in the street who were doing the same thing. I also remembered how when I lived in the flat in Campbell and we didn't have a washing machine my fingers would end up red raw from the rubbing involved in washing my undies by hand.

I may have aspired to a lifestyle beyond my means and upbringing but I didn't want Florrie to do that. I wanted Tambobo to stay exactly as it was. I ignored the fact that the people here were living in poverty, finding it hard to pay for medicines and for their kids' schooling. The biggest smile I ever saw on Batik's face was when he caught a sea snake and sold the skin for ten pesos. I just wanted to be able to come back to Tambobo whenever I could and find it unchanged, like I did after our weekends in Dumaguete.

Every Friday, Batik delivered the four of us across the other side of the bay in his red and white pump boat, named the *RosMariFlor* after his three girls. From there, we caught a pedicab to the main road and then a jeepney to Dumaguete. The first stop for Jen, Karen and me was a beauty salon, where the pedicures and manicures were a glorious treat after a week of saltwater, barnacles and sun. After that, we were ready to party with the Friday Club, a core gathering of about ten Dumaguete gentry, mostly from old Spanish Filipino families except for Robert Si, who was a Filipino Chinese businessman. I wouldn't have been invited through their front doors in Australia or Hong Kong but here, Barry and his yacht and my white skin gave me entrée into their company.

The evening usually started with dinner and then we'd move on to whatever was on offer. Each Friday, one person took responsibility for organising the entertainment. Sometimes we went to a bar, where we smoked cigarettes and joints, drank gin and danced until our feet wore out and the sun threatened to expose us. Another night, a woman old enough to be my grandmother held a party in her house, complete with bar and bartenders, free booze, a dance floor, DJ and disco lights. Then there was the film night where the main screening was *Deep Throat*. Barry set himself up so close to the screen he might as well have been sitting on it. His glasses perched precariously on the end of his nose and he was almost salivating at what was to come. Before the movie was even halfway through, though, he'd fallen asleep. It was my first porn movie and I was surprised at how boring it was.

After these weekends, I was always happy to get back to the simplicity of Tambobo. It reminded me of Coolamon, except that Tambobo's only modern amenity was the flush toilet on *Pegasus* that sent our waste to the bottom of the bay. Being barefoot all the time brought back memories of teasing my toes through the fine chocolate coloured dust in Coolamon's gutters and of paddling in the soft, squidgy mud after a rain. For the first time, I felt glad to be a small town girl, to have something in common with Florrie and her neighbours. They liked Karen and me: we were always ready for a laugh or a chat across the language barrier.

Jen was much more reserved, not what you'd call a warm person. She didn't belly laugh like the rest of us, and she often seemed bored with Barry's antics. She was second-in-command, though, and made sure we knew it. While we were slopping the decks, she'd lie on the bunk and read a book. I was a bit scared of her.

Barry, on the other hand, was all warmth, and he and Karen and I played together like carefree children. It still felt like he was looking beneath my surface and that he liked what he saw. This wisp of a man was helping me get a sense of my shape in the world.

'Look at those muscles,' he said as I rowed him to shore. 'You should see yourself, Di. You're practically vaulting up on deck now. And you leave us all for dead in the water. Have you noticed how we all stick near you when we're swimming ashore? That's because you're the strongest swimmer. I reckon you're the best rower too, of you girls of course. In fact, I've been thinking about anointing you captain of the dinghy.'

'Wow, thanks, I'm honoured. I always wanted to be a captain. So that makes me boss, right? Like you are on the yacht?'

'Yeah, that's right, but don't let the power go to your head or anything.'

'Not like you, no way. But Barry, start bailing will you or we'll never get to shore.'

I loved feeling the strength in my arms when I was rowing, and I was overjoyed that I could do something well. On smooth-water days I could have rowed to China, and on one of those days, when the bay was like a sheet of glass, I managed a magnificent three-sixty-degree turn by miscalculating my stroke by a smidgin of a second.

'Wheee! Look at me! I'm doing an oar-ie!'

'You're easy to live with, you know?' he said to me another day as we sipped our rum and Coke on the bench outside Florrie and Batik's door, where we ended most of our days.

'Really? I'm scared I get in the way too much.'

'In the way? You never get in the way. Those other two are the ones who get in the way. Always where I don't need them to be. Clogging up the stairs, bumping into me. You never do that.'

'I'm always so conscious that I'm much bigger than either of them so I do try to keep out of the way.'

'What do you mean, bigger?'

'You know,' I mumbled. 'Fat. They're both so skinny.'

'Well, yeah, you're right, they're both pretty scrawny, and I wouldn't call you scrawny. But I wouldn't call you fat either. You're how a woman is supposed to be. I like looking at you, that's for sure,' he tittered, leering at me as he dragged on his cigarette.

That sealed it: I would do anything for him.

'Hey, Florrie,' he called. 'Can me and my gorgeous mate here get another rum each, please?'

The days rippled by and every day I felt lighter and happier than the one before. I swam in the warm rain with the kids, bathed at the pump with the women, snorkelled with Barry and wet myself laughing as I watched him drunkenly row the dinghy back to the yacht with it slowly sinking beneath him.

The first crack in paradise came at the end of a day when we were hanging out on Florrie's bench. After a while, Karen and Jen had decided to return to *Pegasus*, and Barry and I sat on, watching the colours thrown against the sky by the setting sun. In the background, I could hear Batik crooning to three-year-old Flora Mae as he rocked her to sleep in her hammock.

'Isn't it marvellous?' I breathed. 'So perfect, so peaceful.'

'It sure is,' mused Barry, running his toes through the dust. 'No claptrap here. We can leave it all behind us.'

'And how lovely is it to not have to be anywhere,' I said, 'to be able to do what we like? Oh, I still find it really hard to believe that it can be like this, that it can be so free and easy.'

'Yeah, we're lucky all right,' agreed Barry.

About half an hour after Karen and Jen left, we heard Jen's voice coming back up the beach.

'Barry!' she yelled, and we saw her marching towards us grim-faced.

'Uh oh,' said Barry under his breath. 'What's the matter, love?' he called.

'I'm sick of it, Barry, really sick of it. What the fuck are you doing? What are you still sitting here for? You've got a boat to look after. You and your little friends!'

Barry and I glanced at each other, dazed by her vehemence.

'Hey, Jen, it's cool. What's going on? Come on, love.' Barry smiled at her.

I expected to see her smile back, for it to have been a joke, but then I saw the glare in her narrowed eyes. I didn't move, or say anything. Raised voices paralysed me. The air around me shivered.

'And as for you!' She moved her steely eyes to me as she picked up a large, empty Coca Cola bottle. Before I knew what had happened, she'd smashed its neck against the bench. Glass flew in all directions and I could feel the barrio behind me holding its collective breath.

Jen, a metre away from me, thrust the jagged bottle in my direction. 'I'd leave now if I were you,' she spat.

I was stunned. I'd never been attacked with such controlled venom before. Angry words were enough to make me shrivel; I could only imagine what a broken Coke bottle could do. My face burned red as my mind tripped over itself trying to find a way out. Seconds passed, the bottle still menacingly pointed at me.

I did the only thing I could think of: I inhaled deeply on my cigarette, blew out the smoke above Jen's head, and said, 'When I finish this cigarette!'

I sucked the guts out of that smoke – surreptitiously – and then I smiled at Barry, forced my legs to move and headed back to the boat. There was nowhere else to go

20

I'd never understood how people continue to co-exist after a loud, nasty battle. As a child, being jolted from sleep by Dad's loud voice and Mum's tears, I was certain my world was coming to an end, but there they'd be at the breakfast table in the morning, not speaking but still in their same seats. In some ways, it's what I'd done too, continuing to adore and pine after Billy even when he was off having sex with other girls, and I'd taken Les back after his golf club fling. I'd thought nothing could save Jacqui and Chen, but if they could still whisper sweet nothings after that frightening mess, then I, surely, could play nicely with Jen.

I was excited to have faced her down, proud that I hadn't skulked away when she brandished broken glass in my face. I could look her in the eyes knowing that she had lost control but I hadn't. She had no power over me: she wasn't my mother. Barry was the one who called the shots on *Pegasus* and he seemed quite happy to keep me on as a crew member.

'Don't worry about Jen. She'll be right, mate.'

Jen must have been fuming – I would have been – but she'd behaved so badly that I didn't care. Barry could have kept things sweet by paying her more attention but he didn't do anything different, and I certainly didn't mind that he joined me doing handstands and turning somersaults in the water with the barrio kids. It was around this time that Jen started drinking and smoking herself into a coma nearly every night.

She was slumbering heavily one Friday night in Dumaguete, in the room the four of us shared at our friend Viv's place behind her optometrist shop. In the early hours of the morning, I woke andced into the kitchen for a glass of water. My Lucas genes never saw me lapse into unconsciousness from drinking but I did get terribly drymouthed. Barry was in the kitchen already, making a cup of tea. After the noise of the disco, it was like sitting in a bubble of silence as we murmured over our steamy cups.

'Good night, hey?'

'Sure was.'

'And what about you? You were dancing up a storm, like a wild thing. You were amazing.'

'Nah, I was just having a good time.'

'Yeah, you were. You're pretty gorgeous, you know.'

'Oh, shut up, Barry.'

We sat close, shoulder to shoulder, heating up the space between us as we joshed and sparked in whispers, then Barry ran his hand down my spine and we stopped laughing. The next minute we were having sex on the kitchen table while the rest of the house slept on. My heart was thumping so hard I was afraid it would wake somebody up. Afterwards, we crept back to the bedroom, Barry resuming his position in bed with Jen, and me on the floor mattress next to Karen. We grinned at each other as the morning light poked its nose through the curtains.

'Di!' said Karen, when I couldn't help but tell her. 'Be careful. Be very, very careful. You know she'll kill you, don't you?'

'Yes, fucking hell, I hope she never finds out.'

Weeks later, when we were anchored in Bio-os, I thought the secret was blown and I expected to die.

Everyone had been glum when Barry decided it was time to leave Tambobo. Our last games of hopscotch with the girls were listless and the barrio was bathed in silence. The chooks didn't even cackle.

'We'll be back,' Karen and I called as *Pegasu*s motored out of the bay.

Little Flora Mae wouldn't look at us, burying her face in her father's neck and six-year-old Mary Joy refused to wave. Lola and Mumma cried. I cried too. Part of me wanted to stay at Tambobo forever, but there was another part of me champing for a new adventure. I was determined to be a good sailor on the seas as well as in the bays, so good that Barry might even ask me to stay on *Pegasus* forever.

My first day of sailing started out fine. The sun beat down gloriously and we stripped off to celebrate. I stood in the bow revelling in the spray as *Pegasus* dipped and climbed with the waves, just a thin steel lifeline between me and the open sea. As the hours wore on and the sun hammered down, my delight came to a sad, ignominious end: the burning rays from above and the sheer radiance blasting back from the water overwhelmed me and I crawled to my bunk sick in the stomach with a fever and a headache that started in my toes. When the sun went down and the air cooled, I'd recovered enough to be above deck, so I was there when, in the dark night, Barry spotted a craft crossing the ocean in front of us and plotted our route to slip past behind it.

'Steam gives way to sail,' he explained, 'but we won't take our chances with this one tonight. Fuck!' he suddenly shouted, and pushed the tiller hard to the left.

His calculations had been good: it was just that the boat we were going to slip behind was towing an unlit barge. If Barry and the nimble *Pegasus* hadn't managed a quick manoeuvre, we would have all ended the day, if we were lucky, clinging onto flotsam in an inky black sea.

With not even twenty-four hours on the water, I was finding that yachting wasn't as much fun, or as glamorous, as I imagined it to be. I was still the little Coolamon scaredy-cat. Not that I needed to worry too much. With Barry, we only sailed from pub to pub: on this first trip, from Florrie's bench to the South Seas Resort Hotel at Dumaguete.

The resort was the kind of place I'd always wanted to stay but could never afford: coconut palms and sun lounges, waiters offering fruit cocktails and beers, and an al fresco dining area that served snacks of chips and spring rolls. I still couldn't afford to stay in a room but we could use the facilities, and sleep on *Pegasus*, sleeps that were becoming increasingly bumpy as *Pegasus* reacted to the rising winds and tide movements we'd been protected from in Tambobo Bay.

One Wednesday morning, I was lying on a sun lounge enjoying the breezes that rustled the coconut palms overhead, sipping on an icy beer, with a well-thumbed copy of *Fear and Loathing in Las Vegas* in one hand and a smoke waiting in the ashtray next to me. I closed the book and lay back, feeling the air caress my face. I heard the clinking as the lunch tables were prepared, and the occasional laugh as the waiters jostled each other.

I'd received a letter that morning from my Forestry mate in Canberra, telling me how cold it was, how busy work had been. I thought of him, in his lab at the CSIRO, and then I thought of Les in Hong Kong, sitting at his desk, chewing his pencil and trying to come up with the best headline ever. My thoughts strayed to all the people I knew who were busy in offices or bustling through their days. I thought of my mother cooking, cleaning, washing, ironing, sewing, serving Meals on Wheels. I thought of her friends in Coolamon doing the same. Deep in my heart, I knew that I really was in paradise, that my fantasy, composted by the women's magazines under Mama's bed, had come true. I was no longer a bystander, not lucky enough, not deserving enough, to have such a life. I had envied the privileges of the people who inhabited the Coolamon Golf Club, those who could afford to go on holidays to Sydney or Queensland, and those who wore clothes that were bought in a shop. I had envied how people who could pay for style and luxury were so much more comfortable in their skin, more confident of their place in the world, so sure their opinions were right. I didn't envy them any more. In fact, I resolved that I would never envy anyone ever again. I held every blissful moment after that lightly, lovingly, no longer searching for something more. I was exuberant as we skinny-dipped with Japanese tourists in the lakes high in the hills separating Negros Oriental from Negros Occidental. When the captain of the USS *Knox*, a proper American navy ship, invited us on an afternoon cruise, the breezes were the balmiest, and the officers were extra-handsome. I enjoyed a sweet fling with one of them: Richard, a beautiful African American sailor who couldn't swim and was scared of the water. He told me he had a wife back in the USA – another one out of my reach, but I was not going to be envious. Not any more.

After a week or so of carousing in Dumaguete, we motored to Bio-os, a long, open beach with nipa houses nestled back towards the road and a couple of well-built uninhabited guesthouses sprawling under the shade trees. Waiting-sheds dotted the beach: pole and roof structures with long nipa tables for sorting fish, sheltering from the rain and sun and, well, waiting – for the day to pass, for the fishermen to come back.

The Bio-os barrio was on the main road to the north of the island, not tucked away in obscurity like Tambobo, and there were a lot more people around: weathered, middle-age fishermen; young spunky fishermen with rippling muscles in sleeveless T-shirts; slow-walking women who swept the beach away from their front doorsteps every morning; and children, a running, laughing, mob of them, who chorused to us every time we came ashore.

'Hello, lady,' they giggled at first. Then, 'Di! Di! Hello! Karen! Hello.'

The barrio of Bio-os was the family fiefdom of the Montenegros. Larry, the son, was a friend, one of the Friday Club founders and regulars. When we went up to his mother's hacienda, we stepped into the world of the landed gentry. Idle young married women clattered mahjong tiles through the afternoon, sipping on gins and smoking cigarettes. We'd sit at the bar watching, enjoying the fan-cooled air. Mrs Montenegro's lips would purse when Karen and I chatted to her housemaids, and they, clad in crisp white uniforms, beamed smiles at us as they swept and served around us. To her credit, Mrs Montenegro resisted sniffing her nose in the air when we arrived and she was a gracious and generous hostess, often inviting us to stay for meals and to sleep over. I understood her snobbery, but I never understood Jen's.

'You shouldn't be hanging around with the staff,' Jen spat. 'It'll just cause problems.'

'She's jealous,' I said to Karen, 'because she hasn't got any friends.'

It was true. As Karen's and my popularity increased, in Dumaguete and at Bio-os, Jen was becoming more and more isolated. While Karen and I were sharing rums and singing in the waiting sheds with young men strumming guitars with missing strings, Jen was hunkered on her bunk or taking solitary trips to Dumaguete.

'*Sigi na! Kanta na!*' the boys would call to me. 'It's your turn now. You sing.'

'No, I can't sing.'

'Of course you can sing, everybody can sing.'

On the morning of my twenty-fourth birthday, I woke at Mrs Montenegro's to Karen gently tweaking my nipple, then spent the day with the rum and songs in the waiting shed, before heading, surprisingly sober, into Dumaguete for a special Friday Club celebration – and they sure knew how to celebrate. As well as the food, the drink, the joints and the dancing, Larry Montenegro had a special birthday surprise for me – a man, Anton, and a night in a hotel.

I was shocked but joined in the laughter, and couldn't see how I could refuse without being thought a prude. I wasn't sure what Larry's gesture meant, though. Did he think I was sex-starved? It was reassuring to know that my occasional bursts of passion with Barry on the verandas of the deserted Bio-os guesthouses were not public knowledge.

After Tambobo, Jen and I had maintained a delicate truce, but the balance was shaken when Barry left on one of his jaunts to Cebu. Karen, Jen and I were taking advantage of our anchorage far from the shore and had stripped naked to wash the deck, diving into the clear waters when we wanted to cool down.

I was leaning against *Pegasus*'s lifeline letting the water drip off me when Jen screeched, 'Arggh, you've got crabs.'

'What? What are crabs?' I asked.

'Those things. There, in your pubic hair. They're crabs. Oh, that's so disgusting. Yuk.'

'It's just sand, isn't it?' I asked as I gingerly fingered through my pubic hair.

'No, they're crabs all right,' said Karen, peering at my crotch.

'You get them from sleeping with someone,' Jen scoffed, 'and anyone else you sleep with will get them too,' she finished triumphantly.

She thought I'd had sex with one of the boys from the beach. Vomit sprang to my throat. The last person I'd had sex with, just a couple of days before, was her boyfriend. Barry would have them, and then she'd get them, and then she'd know, and I would surely die. There was no question about it.

Barry was not due back for at least twenty-four hours and my insides cramped and clutched as my brain feverishly searched for an answer. I knew I had to get to him before he set foot on *Pegasus* so, as soon as the sun rose the next morning, I reeled off a litany of excuses for spending the day ashore.

'I'd like to sit under a palm tree and look at the view from there for a change.'

'I want to take some photos of the kids.'

'Any idea when Barry will get back, Jen?' I asked disinterestedly.

'How would I know? When he's good and ready, I suppose. He mightn't even come back today.'

It was mid-afternoon when I recognised his swagger coming down the path to the beach. I wanted to be one of the kids running to greet him but I just strolled as fast as I could.

'Barry!' I hissed urgently. 'I need to talk to you. I've got crabs.'

'So?' He laughed. 'What's that got to do with me?'

'Barry, I really have them. Crabs!'

'Don't worry about it, Di.'

'Jen says that you only get them from sleeping with someone,' I persisted.

'That's bullshit,' he laughed. 'She's spinning you a line. You can get them from a blanket. Nah, she's just having you on. And, don't worry,' he said, putting his hand on my arm, 'I haven't got them.'

The bubble of hysteria and fear punctured with a crack inside my chest and my legs wobbled as the tension released. I could breathe again. That was one of the longest and scariest days of my life and I had survived it by a whisker. I didn't want to tempt fate.

'We better not do it again, Barry. It's freaked me out too much.'

Our trysts had been getting trickier anyway because of our closer proximity to endless supplies of grog. Barry was often comatose by the end of a night out, slumped on a table in the middle of a disco, or in a chair in someone's lounge room. It became almost impossible to wake him, and Karen and I had to abandon him more than once: one night, in a taxi. By the time the taxi had arrived at our beach, no amount of shaking, pinching, shouting, or rolling Barry's head stirred him and we gave up.

'You'll just have to take him with you,' we told the taxi driver who was on his way home. 'Bring him back in the morning.'

The next morning, I woke up to find Barry looming over me.

'Ha ha! Very funny!'

The taxi had run out of petrol and he had woken up in an abandoned car in a field of sugar cane, almost an hour away from his own bed.

'You'll get yours, don't you worry,' he threatened. 'When you go ashore, you'll get yours.'

For days, I was wary every time I went ashore, taking my lead from the sticker on the mirror in *Pegasus*'s head, which exhorted us to 'Be Alert. Everyone loves a Lert', but nothing happened.

Barry's good humour only failed him once: the night Karen and I sank the dinghy. It was at the end of the day when she and I'd had *Pegasus* to ourselves. We thought we'd surprise Barry and Jen by giving below-deck a really good clean up but fuelled by one joint after the other, and our favourite Kenny Loggins album, we decided to play a trick on Barry instead.

'Let's rearrange his trucking drawer,' we hooted.

The trucking drawer held the camouflage gear for his so-called business trips. We still didn't know what his business was but decided it couldn't have been drugs because he only smoked pot and just the week before I'd nursed a garbage bag full of pungent marijuana heads in a pedicab from Dumaguete to Bio-os.

'Ha! This'll get him,' we laughed, moving the contents from one drawer to another. 'Wait until he sees this.' We didn't know he was planning to go to Cebu the next morning.

Karen and I had dinner with Mrs Montenegro that night and as I was rowing us back to *Pegasus*, the dinghy started taking in more water than usual.

'What are you doing, Kaz? Bail it out. Come on.'

'I can't keep up, Di. Maybe it's sprung another leak. Just hurry up and get us there.'

I hefted the oars furiously and when we reached *Pegasus*, I grabbed hold of her side and held us close. 'Throw our stuff on board. Quick, Karen.'

I was hanging off the side of the yacht, gripping the painter for all my worth, and Karen was standing in knee-high water that gradually rose to thigh-high. As the dinghy sank below the surface, we clung to *Pegasus*, overcome by a fit of the giggles that robbed us of our strength to pull ourselves up and over.

'Let's get Barry,' said Karen, when we finally landed on the deck. 'He'll help us haul it up.'

But Barry was in no mood to help. 'Fix it,' he growled. 'No, I'm not bloody helping you. You mess with my gear and now this? You deal with it. I'm off to Cebu in the morning, early. Just get it done.'

'Oh, Barry, come on. You know we can't do it ourselves.'

'You damn well work out how. And I want it ready to go when the sun comes up. Go on. Fix it.'

There was no way that Karen and I could lift the dinghy ourselves so we had to swim it to shore.

'Bloody bastard,' Karen grumbled. 'He could have helped. Why's he in such a bad mood?'

'Did you see his face?' I chortled. 'God, I've laughed so much today. What's that saying? Laugh in the face of adversity? That's going to be my motto from now on.'

We dragged the upside-down vacuum-sealed dinghy up to the water's edge, where we used the waves and sand to help unglue its face from the planet.

'Let's swim it back,' I suggested. 'I don't want to go through that again and it'll get him to shore at least, if he goes by himself.'

It was one of those nights when the sky was bursting with stars and the moon rested fully content on the horizon like a just-fed baby. It was another tourist brochure moment, especially when a fishing boat slid gracefully across the moon's face, the oarsman standing sentinel sweeping them along.

That was to be my last magical moment. Within the week, there wasn't much to laugh about.

21

While Barry was still away, Karen and I went on an overnight visit to Tambobo to see Florrie's family and to be at the christening of her new baby, Dennis. When we arrived back at the yacht, Barry was still in Cebu and Jen was nowhere to be found.

'She went to Dumaguete,' chorused the kids. 'Back tomorrow maybe.'

Up at the Montenegro hacienda, Karen and I happily accepted Mrs Montenegro's offer of dinner. When we were heading back to the beach, the wind had risen but we heard music and laughter coming from the kitchen, so we poked our heads in.

'Come in, come in,' they cried. 'Come and join us.'

There was a guitar, with most of its strings, and a Beatles songbook. How could we refuse? We slid onto a bench at the table and sang with them, through every song in the book.

'You know so many,' they laughed with surprise.

Karen and I decided to sleep the night in a beach shelter instead of on *Pegasus*, but with the wind increasing and not knowing what arrangements Jen had made, we thought we'd better check the boat first. The beach was deserted, so we stripped down to our underpants and swam out, pulling ourselves up onto the deck before we realised there were a couple of teenage boys lounging against the sails. They jumped up, eyes popping out of their heads. Wide grins spread across their faces as they gaped at our big white breasts gleaming in the moonlight. Andrelito and Dwight had been tasked with looking after the boat and, after this moonlight meeting, they looked after us as well, our unofficial bodyguards. It seemed a joke at the time.

The people clumped on the beach next morning looked serious. 'There's a big storm coming. It'll hit this afternoon. Very big. Not good at all.'

Out on the yacht, there was confusion. Somehow, in the night, the anchor rope and chains had become twisted and by the time we boarded in the ominous morning light, the anchor was missing. Missing! And the sea was getting stormier by the minute.

'What are we supposed to do?' we wailed. 'Where the fuck is Barry? Where's Jen?'

'How do you lose a bloody anchor? Are we sure it's gone?'

Some of the men helped us rig up another anchor, all of us hoping that an anchor for a fifteen-foot fishing boat would hold *Pegasus*'s thirty-five-feet in whatever was to come. The men watched the horizon constantly, working frantically to finish. They had their own places to secure as well.

Finally, they'd done all they could do and hurried us into their boats. 'You can't stay here. It's too dangerous. You have to come with us. Big storm and big waves. Quick. Come now.'

Karen and I stood on the veranda of a beach hut as the typhoon hit, and watched the churning sea and blasting wind throw *Pegasus* up and down and down and up, spinning her around this way then that. She was blown onto her side, her mast dipping into the frothing, hostile waters. Tears streamed down my face and I crossed my fingers, praying that she would right herself. Then up she'd surge and jump about before the next dunking. The makeshift anchor held for a while but then, in the blink of an eye, *Pegasus* was riding the waves towards the beach. We all watched, horrified, as she hit the shallows. When she careened herself on a sandy-bottomed section free from any rock hazards, we shouted with relief.

The wind dropped suddenly and it was eerily still. Karen and I hugged each other.

'No, not finished,' the men said. 'It will come back. This is just the middle of it. Come on. We must empty the boat.'

We ran with them, straining to listen to their advice, to decipher the translations by boys who spoke only a little more English than their seasoned boat-in-storm experts. A chain of women, men and children removed everything of any value or usefulness to the safety of a beach shelter. Only the steadiest and most reverent hands were allowed to carry the sextant, an awesome object to men who were more used to navigating by the stars and sun. Then, with the rain pelting down, we worked alongside the men to secure *Pegasus* to the strongest coconut palm within roping distance. The incoming tide was a danger. Bouncing around on the sandy seabed could break up the beautiful wooden hull that we'd spent hours scraping free of barnacles. With each incoming wave, we pulled on the rope to keep *Pegasus* wedged on the bottom, praying the coconut palm would stand fast.

Jen arrived back from Dumaguete in the middle of the toil and stood watching from a shelter.

A few hours later when the tide was on the turn, we did the opposite. While Jen slept on her bunk, Karen and I, with our new friends, Andrelito, Dwight, and Pedrito, nursed *Pegasus* through the stormy night, gradually playing out the rope to keep her afloat on the retreating tide. In bikinis and sun hats, and fuelled by joints, we held a Mad Hatter's tea party, complete with china teacups and crooked little fingers. The boys were agog and laughed along with us as tears of hysteria spilled from our eyes and mingled with the rain thrashing down.

*

After the typhoon, nothing looked the same. The coconut palms hung with shredded crowns; palm fronds, coconut husks, driftwood, dead birds and dead fish had been blasted along the beach, across the road and into the hinterland. Nipa huts sagged, their thatching dishevelled or missing. The sea, once a waveless expanse protected by the outer Philippine islands, now resembled an Australian beach with waves pounding in. The spume and water had colonised more of the sand and it looked like they planned to stay. The air itself felt sharper, less magical, less vibrant. On the beach, the kids played more quietly, casting anxious glances out to sea, like children confused by a parents' inexplicable rage.

Pegasus's crew came through the maelstrom bedraggled and sagging as well, and the tenuous threads that had held us together for the past five months, ended up with the flotsam strewn inland. It was as if everybody had been washed away: Karen spent most of her days ashore with Pedrito; Jen spent more and more time in Dumaguete; and Barry, who had returned after the drama subsided, had headed back to Cebu within a couple of days

I was the only one with nowhere to go and, as I sat on *Pegasus* with nobody else in cooee, I felt abandoned. My joy at helping save *Pegasus* leaked into the silence. When the sky darkened and the breezes picked up, heralding another storm, my fears swelled with the ocean and angry tears coursed down my cheeks. Where are they? They should be here. What if the new anchor doesn't hold? What if it's another big storm?

After checking the anchor chain was still taut and checking the deck was clear, there was nothing I could do but wait. As the squall came in, I went below and stroked the varnished timbers, feeling helpless and sad – for *Pegasus,* and for myself. After months of bliss and tumult, of hard physical yakka, and hanging-out, I was alone again, still not particularly special to anybody. I recognised the slippery-dip at the end of that thought and I hesitated, remembering the day at the South Seas Resort Hotel when I'd resolved to never envy anyone ever again. Stepping onto that slide would make that resolution null and void, and it had felt so good. I wanted to be a woman who didn't panic at the first sniff of solitude so, if it didn't come naturally, I would pretend: I would relax.

I ran my fingers across the books in our limited library for the umpteenth time. Damn, I'd read them all but one and it was a non-fiction. The book I'd borrowed from the Hong Kong library about Japanese Buddhism hadn't inspired me to read any more non-fiction. Give me a spy novel or a Jane Austen any day. But, with the rain lashing down, there was nothing else to do so I reluctantly pulled it from the shelf. It was written by Susan Brownmiller and was called *Against Our Will.* I had no idea as I looked at its cover that a different sort of typhoon was heading my way.

Against Our Will was about rape. Why would I want to read this? I didn't know anybody who'd been raped. Well, it'll get me through the next few hours, I supposed, so I started reading.

All I knew about rape was that rapists were evil, psychopathic maniacs, like the one in *The Boston Strangler*, a book that had so terrified and nauseated me when I was fourteen. My interest was piqued when Susan Brownmiller said she'd thought that too, until she heard women talking about what men in their life had done to them, and that was why she'd written the book.

I read on. It's not just psychotic maniacs who rape women, she wrote. Ever since some prehistoric man discovered he could force a woman to have sex with him, and that he felt really powerful when he did, men have been raping women or threatening them with rape. As a result, women are afraid of men and easier to control.

Whoa, I breathed, putting the book down. What does that even mean?

There was a distant rumble of thunder and I poked my head through the hatch to check what was happening. The rain had lightened and *Pegasus* was steady.

Is she right? I wondered, slipping back on to the bunk. Are we all afraid of men? Isn't it just dark alleys and strangers that we have to be scared of? And if we are afraid, does that make us easier to control?

For a long time, I'd thought that the idea of a woman belonging to a man was pretty stupid, but I didn't think it warranted marching in the street about or burning our bras. Maybe it did, though. Thinking back on how I was around men, I realised that I felt a lot safer with them when it was obvious that I was already with someone. With another man.

When I was growing up, my mother had hinted at terrible things that could happen to girls who weren't good but I'd always felt safe in Coolamon. I never thought anything would happen to me because of who my father and grandfather were. For the short time with Billy by my side, I'd felt safe too: nobody would touch his girlfriend if that's what I was. Even so, I made sure that I was always polite and said hello and smiled at everyone. I thought if they liked me then I was sure to be safe too. Did that mean I was afraid of them all?

A wave sloshed against the side of the boat and through the porthole of the bunk I saw that it was still showering softly, soothing the earth after the previous rampage, like a mother gently rubbing bruise cream on the wounds she'd inflicted. I lit a cigarette, picked up the book and opened to where I'd left off, thoughts and smoke swirling around me.

Brownmiller went on to say that men stayed in control not just by raping and scaring women, but also by pitting women against each other. When I read that, an arrow went straight into my gut: it was true. I don't know if I was 'pitted against' other girls but I thought about how dismissive I was of girls who huddled together discussing haircuts and nail polish. It was the blokes' conversations I'd always wanted to be a part of: who was the best on the cricket team, whether the footy ref was biased, when was the bloody rain going to come, and who do those politicians think they are anyway? With a jolt, I realised how disdainful I was of all the work that women like my mother did to keep everybody fed and clothed, and how I knew from an early age that real power sat in the front bar at the pub and not at home in the kitchen. I knew that even though Mum was the one who had always wielded the strap, Dad was the boss of us all, the one who could bring my terrifying mother to tears. How did it make her feel, I wondered, to have so much power over us kids, but none in the rest of her life? How did she feel about me wanting to be Daddy's girl, his Chicken, not hers? My face flushed as I recognised myself as a woman who had been suckered into believing that men were better than women. Or was it just that I thought they had better lives? I wondered whether I wanted the same power as a man, or just to be with a man who had power.

I stretched back on the cushions and closed my eyes, letting the pages fall shut. I felt confusion wash over me. My thoughts were jumbled and it was hard to catch just one. Images of men I'd had sex with flashed through my brain.

Could any of the things that happened to me be called rape? They weren't in alleyways, and they weren't complete strangers. There were no guns or knives involved. The first time was the bloke from the Wello pub when I'd only been in Canberra a week and was really drunk for the first time in my life. Could you call that rape? Whether it was or not, it felt like it, and that man tore apart more than my hymen. Something else had pooled with the blood on the sheets that night: my trust that I would lose my virginity to a man who loved me. It didn't seem to matter any more after that and so I'd slept with lots of different men. Was I just looking for someone to keep me safe?

Huddled on *Pegasus*'s bunk in the Philippines, I finally understood what that man had meant when he called out across the bar, 'I broke her.' My will had been broken; I'd been brought under control. But it hadn't been enough for just one man to give me the message.

There was the man who took me to the posh restaurant on Canberra's Red Hill and forced me to understand that I owed him sex for the fancy dinner he'd bought me. Was that rape? There was Carolyn's boyfriend's housemate who had got into bed with me in the middle of the night and tried to have sex with me. Would that have been rape? I thought about all the other times I'd had sex when I didn't want to, even with Les when I was too tired or drunk. I never wanted to cause a scene; I didn't know how they might react. Buried deep in my gut, I just knew that I had to keep them happy or something bad might happen. After that first time, I'd stopped believing that I had any right to refuse, especially after I went on the Pill. It was just easier to give in and do it.

I cried then – great wailing howls, about how stupid and naïve I'd been, how ashamed I was, how sick I felt. I cried with sadness for the young woman I'd been and how badly I'd let her be treated. I cried until I couldn't breathe for the snot. The afternoon light was fading, and I was exhausted. My throat was raw from chain-smoking and I felt as if I'd been pounded against the sand by storm waves and was struggling to catch my breath.

When I finally surfaced, the world looked different, like it did after the tornado: shiny clean but with its secrets scattered haphazardly across the beach, the minutiae of life displaced for all to see. And like after the storm, when everything seemed quiet and calm, the waves kept rolling in for weeks afterwards, dumping debris that I'd not noticed before.

I was hit by one in our favourite Dumaguete breakfast restaurant when a man I barely knew asked if he could talk to me privately, and there, in the room next to my friends, with the door ajar, he tried to force me to have sex. I hadn't yet learned the skill of yelling out – it would have been too embarrassing – but I did manage to escape him and get back to my friends, where I pretended nothing had happened.

Another wave crashed when Marty, a Friday Club acquaintance, invited me to his family house in the hills to escape the heat. I accepted gladly, only to discover his family weren't there but three of his friends were. Using all the tact and wiles I could muster, I managed to persuade him that no, I didn't want to have sex with any of them, and to drive me back to town, please.

Then there was another acquaintance I'd known for a whole thirty minutes who'd pulled me aside at a friend's house. 'Do you mind if I ask you a personal question?' he said.

'Sure,' I replied, 'go ahead.'

'Will you go to bed with me?'

My body had flushed and stiffened but I was conscious of not wanting to hurt his feelings.

One night, when I was sleeping at Mrs Montenegro's, I jerked awake certain that someone had sat down on the bed and started touching me, but there was nobody there.

'That would be my father,' laughed Larry when I told him. 'He was always a lusty old man.'

Apparently even dead men could make waves.

The waves became particularly tempestuous when Karen and I went to a barrio dance with Mrs Montenegro's workers. My skin prickled at the menace in the heavy air.

'We have to leave,' said Pedrito, ushering us out quickly. 'There's no respect here.'

Later, he told us that someone had been stabbed and it had something to do with Karen and me. I didn't know whether to believe him or not. I didn't know whether to believe Barry either when he told us that even at Tambobo it hadn't always been safe for us, that he'd paid Batik to protect us whenever a fishing boat swarming with young testosterone-filled men sought shelter there.

'Batik lurked in the bushes with a machete,' said Barry. 'You girls would have been fair game. What did you expect?'

Were we part of the problem, then? I loved the sun on my bare skin – the fewer clothes the better – but maybe my short skirts and shorts, my sarongs and crop tops, as well as my friendliness, were taken the wrong way.

The new world I was seeing had a sordid tinge, just like the typhoon-ravaged beach at Bio-os. My glossy idyll was coming to an end, and as Barry sank deeper into an alcohol-and-drug-fuelled haze, and was often absent, even *Pegasus* was losing her charm. Still, it was bloody hard to make the decision to leave and, finally, it was Jen whose rage threw us up on the water's edge with the wreckage from the storm.

She tried to get rid of us a few weeks after the typhoon, by threatening Karen with a knife.

'Oh, I don't care, Di,' Karen said. 'She's losing the plot. Don't worry about her.'

It must have really got up Jen's nose when Karen ignored her, and a few days later she tried again, this time in Mrs Montenegro's dining room. She waited at least until our hostess had retired for the night.

'What is it with you two?' she snarled, after Karen and I had been bantering with Betty, who collected the dishes and wiped the table. 'Can't you just ignore these people? You don't have to be friends with everyone. And you, Karen,' she said, rolling her eyes. 'You and Pedrito. That's just disgusting.'

'Oh, shut up, Jen,' said Karen wearily. 'Pass me the sugar, Di.'

'No, I won't shut up. You're just a slut.' Jen's voice rose and her face mottled red. She stood up and leaned over the table at Karen. 'All you think about is what's between your legs,' she sneered. 'A beach boy, for god's sake. You've got no class, or taste.'

'Jen, shut up,' I said. 'Don't go on. It's boring.'

She turned to me, her sneer widening. 'And you,' she spat, 'don't tell me you didn't want to sleep with him too. How'd you feel when Karen got him? Huh?' She grinned at me then, like she had delivered the ultimate insult.

My pulse thumped in my head as I slowly pulled myself to my feet and leaned towards her, grinning back. 'And what makes you think Karen got in first, Jen?'

That shut her up, but we were all sick of each other. Too much energy was being wasted trying to hold back the inevitable. The next day, Karen and I moved our gear from the boat to the beach, where we slept on the tables in a waiting-shed for another week while we made our plans for returning to Hong Kong.

Jen looked like thunder every time she came ashore and saw us still there.

The kids ran up to her, clapping their hands and laughing. 'Jennifer! Jennifer! *Sigi na! Kanta na!*'

Scowling fiercely, she batted them away like they were mosquitoes.

Barry came back from Cebu before we left and there was a farewell party for us in Dumaguete. He even made an effort to stay awake.

'I'm going to miss you, Di. You're fun to have around, most of the time,' he snickered. 'We won't mention the taxi or my trucking drawer. We get on pretty good, don't we?'

'We do, Barry,' and we nudged each other, laughing.

'Not much of a sailor, though, are you?' he tittered again. 'Keep in touch, Di. Please. Write to me. I'll let you know where we are.'

'I'd love to. Thanks, Barry. Thanks for inviting me. I really mean it. I have had the most amazing time. I feel like I can handle anything.'

A month after the typhoon, I was on a plane that jumped and

bucked its way to Hong Kong. For a fleeting moment, I hated Jen, but I knew she didn't matter any more: nothing would change the fact that, for a while, I had been in paradise. I'd fallen crazily in love with coconuts and beaches, the sun and the sea, with sarongs and thongs, with laughing and talking all day – always laughing and talking. Every morning I'd woken up happy and I didn't envy anyone else in the world. I had stood naked in the rain and in the sea spray as *Pegasus* rode the waves. I had danced on the beach with children and in the discos with my friends. I had drunk rum and Coke and gin and tonics, eaten liver barbecues from street stalls, and smoked copious numbers of joints, which felt so good I swore I'd never drink again. I'd been introduced to hedonism and embraced it heartily.

I had discovered, too, that even in paradise it can storm and rage. The typhoon had given *Pegasus* a dunking and Susan Brownmiller had given me one. She had held up a mirror, and while I didn't like all that I saw, at least I now had a sense of my edges. I had arrived in Tambobo uncertain of them, not knowing where I began or where I ended. I was leaving, feeling strong for the first time in my life: I had never been so thin, and my skin glowed with a golden tan. I was no longer the scaredy-cat girl from Coolamon.

22

Four months later, I pulled down the top of the carriage window as my train shuffled away from Coolamon. I was heading back to Canberra, determined, once again, to start a new life, to leave behind the confusion and self-destructive behaviours of my youth, to be the woman I wanted to be.

A wave of hot air flowed into the carriage and I stretched my face towards it, breathing in the familiar scorching smell of summer grasses. My eyes tracked along the road running beside the train and I thought about all the other times I'd made the trip in this direction: tucked up in my pyjamas on the back seat of Mama's black FJ on our pre-dawn departure to Aunty Gene's wedding in Sydney; scrabbling to sit next to Helen on the exuberant train trip with our fourth form class to a vocational guidance camp at Narrabeen, the first time many of us had been away without family – for some, their first trip away from Coolamon; and then that blurry drive to Canberra with my parents at the end of sixth form when I thought that life had to be better anywhere but Coolamon.

'Coolamon?' I used to say to city friends. 'Phhht! There's nothing to see there.'

Before I made my resolution not to envy anyone ever again, I'd envied everyone: people who lived watching the tides wax and wane, those who lived where mountain peaks speared through clouds, even those who came from the flatter, dustier, hotter lands. I'd been especially envious of people whose natural habitat was among tower blocks and bustling streets. Now, after living in the concrete towers of Hong Kong, being in the paradise of coconut trees and blue waters at Tambobo, and surviving the typhoon ravages of Bio-os, I knew in my bones that it wouldn't matter where else I lived – Coolamon, where I knew the feel of the soft gutter dirt under my feet, would always be my home, even when the sharp pain of the bindi-eyes pierced my heels. Its thorns, and its naivety, would always be with me. Surely only a Coolamon girl would have smuggled marijuana between the Philippines and Hong Kong in a talcum powder container. It was so tainted by the too-sweet perfume it was unsmokeable. As the town receded behind me, I knew I would always be a country town girl, a Coolamon girl, but I also knew that I could never live there again.

I'd gone over to Coolamon to clean Mama's house while she was at my uncle's place in Newcastle recuperating from a stroke she'd suffered after our family Christmas in Huskisson. I can't say it was the family gathering that caused her blood to clot but it wouldn't have helped: there was always some tension when she and Mum were in the same house…and when Mum and I were in the same house.

Even when I'd walked through my parents' front door in Huskisson after being away for two years, there had been the familiar sting of my mother's hand on my bare arm.

'For heaven's sake, Dianne,' she'd said as she struck. 'It's obvious you haven't got any more sense into that head of yours. What on earth gets into you?'

'I just wanted to surprise you,' I said, pushing back my tears and trying to keep my voice from wobbling.

'That's just like you. Only worried about yourself,' she grumbled, wiping her hands on her apron. 'It's about time you started thinking about other people. I suppose she just expected you to drop everything to pick her up,' she said to my old CSIRO friend, Robin, who'd driven me down from Sydney airport. 'What are we going to do with her?'

Rob shuffled his feet, threw me a glance and laughed self-consciously. 'I'm glad to see her back,' he said.

'Hmmph!' she'd snorted derisively.

I'd been living out of home for seven years but within moments back in her house, I felt reduced to the cowering child in the laundry again. Then came Christmas…

I was setting the table one night while Dad was pouring shandies, Mum was stirring the gravy, and Mama was cleaning up the sink. There was a peaceful hum and I'd felt a flush of warmth at being back in my family's bosom.

'Where would you like me to put this, Audry?' Mama had asked, scooping up the vegetable scraps into a colander.

'Just pop them on the washing machine and I'll take it out to the chooks later,' Mum replied.

'It's a small laundry, isn't it?' Mama commented. 'Not like they used to make them. You could have a party in mine.'

'That's something I miss,' sighed Mum. 'Our laundry in Coolamon. That floor was so cool in summer. Remember, Dianne, when I'd give Lassie an ice cube on a hot day? She'd try and hold it with her paws, chasing it around the floor and licking it until the whole thing was gone.'

'What I remember,' I said, 'is that I was usually in the laundry cleaning my shoes when you found out I'd done something wrong and came in with the strap.'

'Oh, Dianne, that's not true,' my mother burst out. 'How can you say that?'

'It's true, Mum, but it's okay.'

'Oh, God!' she moaned, tears starting to roll down her cheeks. She threw down the spoon and ran out of the kitchen, through the laundry and into the backyard, letting the screen door bang behind her.

Dad and Mama pointed their eyes at me, silently.

'It's just how I remember it,' I explained, shrugging.

'Well, you better go after her,' said Dad. 'Go and apologise. Bring her back in. Go on.'

Reluctantly, I'd entered the dark backyard. I couldn't see my mother amongst the looming shapes of the shrubs and trees but I heard her sobbing breaths coming from the far corner, where the chooks and ducks lived. I dragged my feet there.

Just say sorry and it'll be okay, I told myself. It doesn't have to mean anything.

And I was sorry, but not for the right reasons: I was sorry because I had to say sorry, and I was sorry that my words had got me into this predicament.

'Sorry, Mum,' I mumbled. 'I didn't mean to upset you. It's just what I remember.'

'Oh, Dianne. How could you? That was a horrible thing to say. It wasn't like that.'

'I'm sorry. Come on. Come inside.'

I took her arm and led her down the yard, through the laundry and into the brightly lit kitchen.

While I was in Coolamon this time, I'd stood outside my childhood home yearning to see into its bones. The tall pencil pine was still inside the driveway gate, and the lantana flowered red and orange beneath my parents' bedroom window but I couldn't see if the laundry still had its smooth concrete tubs, if the step from the lounge room into the back veranda was still worn down. Was the fibro door into the backyard still warped? Did the peach trees still bear too much fruit? Was the grapevine, with the furry black caterpillars that Paul used to push under the toilet door at me, still lining the path to the back gate? Were the same orange trees in the chook yards? Was there a woodpile beside the garage?

Tears had filled my eyes as I realised how lightly I'd left it when I first moved to Canberra. I'd just taken for granted that my childhood home would always be there for me. I wished I'd paid more attention to the doors with their high round handles, the camphor smell in the sleepout cupboard, how the walls creaked when the wind blew, the rattle of the double doors into the lounge room, and the sunlight bouncing off the kitchen table lighting up the lino tiles. I wanted to walk through the front gate again. It still bore the name Kelvin in ironwork – whoever Kelvin was: I never knew. The shady front veranda, where I seemed to stub my toe every day when I was little, beckoned. If only I could lean against the veranda railing like I'd done with Billy and Chris the day of the 1972 election. Now, it seemed like the most normal thing in the world for us to have done, but it had only been possible because my mother wasn't at home.

At Mama's house, I scoured it from top to bottom: the fancy teapots on the shelves that never got used except to collect dust, the plates and bowls stacked behind the cupboard doors, the cutlery in the top drawer and the implements in the stuffed-full second drawer. I sorted rubber bands and loose screws in the bottom drawer. I washed all the knick-knacks through the house and explored the top shelves of the cupboards in the girls' room. Every surface sparkled after I'd been at it. The hoovering took years off the carpet and I sucked up the loose grit from the cracks in the pisé walls. I disposed of moth-eaten mice from under the cabinet in the front lounge room and sad, dead sparrows that had taken a dive down the chimney. As I scrubbed the bathroom, I remembered being very, very young and Mama bathing me one-handed because she'd sprained her wrist. When I needed a break, I sat on the front veranda with a cup of tea and listened to the summer insects buzzing in the silence.

I wished Helen was home too. It had been so exciting when I saw her in Sydney a few weeks earlier. I had been as nervy as a puppy, wondering what it would be like between us after the longest separation we'd had since I was in my bassinet and she was in her pram. Would it be different? It wasn't: she was still my best friend and I was still me – in awe of her, gawky and self-conscious, worried I'd say or do something stupid and she wouldn't like me any more. Being with your best friend should be like being in your most snuggly pyjamas and dressing gown but, except for brief snatches, it hadn't been like that with us since hormones and self-consciousness became part of the high school curriculum. I wanted it back again, and was sure we'd find it as we wandered the back lanes around the showground and visited the cemetery to see the new lawn section the council had made, just like the one we'd dreamed about when we were regulars there. Maybe we would do it one day but, after this trip, I knew it wouldn't be for a long time.

A shrill whistle jerked me back to the train. We were going through one of the dangerous (for cars) S-bend crossings that punctuated the stretch of road between Coolamon and Cootamundra. I was surprised to find myself still standing at the window, my bag over my shoulder. I slumped down into my seat, thankful that the carriage was so empty. My chest was tight and I breathed shallowly. I didn't want to disturb the emotions lurking beneath. I didn't want to cry.

Billy had found me on Mama's front veranda within hours of my arrival, the curious telepathic connection between us proving itself again, or else it was a really, really, small town.

'G'day,' he said, grinning as he stepped over the low front gate. 'You're back again.'

'Hi,' I managed to reply as a thousand fluttering wings clogged my chest and throat.

'It's been a long time. You've been away?'

'Yep,' I said. 'To Hong Kong. And I spent some time in the Philippines.'

'What was it like?'

'Oh, it was okay. Hong Kong was pretty exciting. For a while. But then it got overwhelming. It's just so busy. The Philippines was great. Quieter. Lots of sun, blue skies. Coconut trees. After being there I didn't cope real well back in Hong Kong. Money and concrete. That's what it's all about. Not my sort of place. Do you know, there are roads that are built up high off the ground that pass within feet of blocks of flats where people are eating and sleeping.'

'Not like here then,' he mused.

'No, not like here.'

'You still with that bloke? Les?'

'Nah. We broke up about six months after we got to Hong Kong.'

'That's no good.'

'Oh well, he got me there, I guess, and if we hadn't broken up, I wouldn't have gone to the Philippines. I loved it there. So, what's been happening here?'

'Nothing much,' he grinned.

Billy came past after work each day that week, and for the first time in my Coolamon life I didn't have to keep alert in case someone was watching me. Apart from Paul, who worked out on a farm, I was alone: no parents, no parents' friends, no grandparents.

Some afternoons we sat with our feet propped up on the low brick wall of Mama's veranda watching the commuters arriving back from Wagga, the sun glowing golden in the west. One day, we met instead at the corner pub where Pa used to drink.

It was as intense between us as it always had been. When our arms touched, electricity sparked through me but it didn't feel so dangerous now that my body was feeling more solid, more experienced in the world. I still thrilled at sitting beside him, though, especially without the desperation of my teenage years.

Another night, for old times' sake, we met at the golf club, where we sat in a corner and reminisced about the dances we went to after the footy games.

'You were my first date,' I told him.

'Yeah, well, we should've had more,' he said smiling at me. 'Your father was always propped up at the bar over there though. Watching me the whole time.'

'Thank God, those days are over,' I laughed.

'Really?' he asked, brushing my hand.

I glanced at him and our eyes stuck. They wouldn't let go. Next minute, our little fingers had found each other and soon all our fingers had followed suit. My heart skipped and I was glad the bar was almost empty. We were in a bubble, just looking at each other.

'Do you want to go?' he asked, and I nodded silently.

The bubble floated us out of the club and into Mama's two-tone beige EJ Holden.

'Shall we just go for a drive?' I suggested, my pulse drumming in my ears.

'Sure.'

My hands shook as I steered Mama's car through the moonless night along the roads skirting our end of town. I didn't dare look at him, just kept my eyes fixed on where the headlights lit up the scrub.

Somewhere near the cemetery – where else? I always went there when I came back to town – I juddered the car to a stop and we turned to face each other. I was looking into his eyes, the ones I'd drowned in years before. We reached for each other at the same time and it was like slipping into my most comfortable dress, it felt so right. We couldn't seem to get close enough until, in the blink of an eye, we were making love. Something unleashed inside me that night, part of me that had been chained up for too long. I wanted to howl my joy to the moon. This was what I'd always wanted – to be this close to him. How I'd longed for him to love me like I'd loved him. I wanted to believe he had: I told my Canberra friends we were star-crossed lovers, like the ones Neil Sedaka sang about. I wanted to believe it when he haunted my dreams and I woke up from them with an aching heart. I wanted this night with the darkness surrounding us to last forever. But bubbles always burst.

I dropped him off near his house, where, I had conveniently forgotten, he was a partner and a father. I could barely change the gears to cross the railway line: my arms were weightless, liquefied. My stomach was in chaos, though. Hysterical laughter and disbelief bubbled beneath the surface: I had just made love with Billy Marshall on the beige-towelling front seat of my grandmother's car.

In the morning, I was still jumping out of my skin when I walked up the street to get some more Ajax. Outside the Co-op, the only grocery shop left since Iverach's shut down, I ran into Valda, one of my kindergarten to sixth form schoolmates. I stayed at her farm sometimes when we were in primary school and she was the most popular and prettiest of us girls until Helen took over. When she married her childhood sweetheart, it was one of the first weddings Les and I went to.

'How's Tony?' I asked.

'He's good. How was your trip?'

It was going to be a hot day and the veranda blinds were down on the other side of the street to block the morning sun. A few cars puttered their noses into the kerb near us. We waved and said hello to the few we'd known all our lives. As we chatted, I idly watched a woman I'd never seen before pushing a pram up the street towards us. There was another littlie holding onto its side.

'Have you seen Helen since you've been back?' Valda asked.

'Yep. She's good.'

The woman with the pram was staring at us as she came closer. I turned my eyes back to Valda: I didn't want a stranger to think I was rude.

'How are your parents?' I asked, as the pram came level with us.

Suddenly, there was the harsh blast of a furnace at my back and the world faltered on its axis.

'Are you the tart that's been screwing Billy Marshall?'

Valda gasped.

The heat of shame flooded me but my blood froze. My whole body turned to ice. I couldn't move. I couldn't speak. All the words I knew stampeded through my brain. Valda stood silently, looking from me to the other woman and back at me, waiting to see what was going to happen. I wanted to laugh and weep at the same time. This was just my bloody luck. Nothing had changed. I'd never been able to do anything in Coolamon without being found out and, now, the one thing I'd dreamed about for years had happened and I didn't even get twenty-four hours to savour it.

'I'm not a tart,' was all I managed to stutter.

'Well, you can have him,' she spat, her face pale and tight with anger. 'I don't want him.'

She turned and gave the pram an angry push past us. The little one holding on looked back at us with big eyes as she yanked at his hand.

Her words sent an electric shock to my brain, rearranging the neurons. I could have what had been a deep desire for so long but I needed to make a split-second decision. There was no time for mucking around. A choice had been laid out before me. The euphoria of my bubble pooled in the gutter. My actions had consequences. My next move had implications for this woman I didn't know and, from the looks of it, for at least two children.

I watched a flock of birds wheeling lazily in the sky, as the train clack-clacked its way through a red-dirt cutting. Had it only been yesterday? I remembered the sun beating down on me as I stood in front of the Co-op, the sharp silence in the street, how it had felt like all the air had been sucked out of my world. As the mother of Billy's children continued up the footpath, it was as if time had stopped, and what popped into my brain had been the book Karen had given to me when she'd come to a women's refuge conference in Canberra not long after I arrived back from Hong Kong.

'You've got to read it,' she'd said, handing me a well-thumbed paperback copy of *The Women's Room* by Marilyn French. 'You'll love it.'

On the cover, it said 'this novel changes lives' and she was right: I had loved it. It had been like reading Susan Brownmiller again except it was a novel. I was excited by the idea of women being strong and independent, not needing men in their lives. Susan Brownmiller's *Against Our Will* was an alarm clock that had been ticking since the day I sat on the boat alone at Bio-os, and it was Marilyn French who'd set it off. There were a couple of sentences buried deep within one of the chapters that had triggered a spontaneous gusher of sobs to burst from my throat.

Love, is insanity, she had written. It is the taking of a rational and lucid mind by delusion and self-destruction. You lose yourself, you have no power over yourself, you can't even think straight.

As the train rattled along, I felt again the ache where those words had punched into my chest. They'd caused me to see how desperate I'd always been for someone to love me, how after moving to Canberra I convinced myself I was in love with anybody who showed the least bit of interest. I'd tried to be the woman they would want to be with but I never could be. Not even with Les. Maybe if I'd had a clearer idea about who I was or what I thought or what I wanted it would have been different. But there was just a gaping emptiness inside that I tried to fill with alcohol, drugs and sex. It was pure luck that I'd survived: all those nights spent in a swirl of alcohol, the times I'd driven when the road swam in front of me, and too many edgy flings with men who didn't give a fuck and, if they did, they certainly didn't wear a condom.

That gusher of sobs had scoured me raw and I'd felt that I could never return to the person I'd been before. But I must have hit the snooze button. The jangling alarm had gone off again, this time in the middle of Coolamon's main street.

In Marilyn French's book, it was clear that women had to look out for each other. And I hadn't done that. Was that who I wanted to be? Who did I want to be? Did I want to live in Coolamon? Did I want to be with Billy? All this raced through my brain in a matter of seconds until suddenly I felt certain. I loved Billy as much as I always had, but it was too late. We both had other lives. He had children, a partner and a life in Coolamon; I'd lived in Hong Kong, the Philippines and Canberra, and I knew that I wanted more for myself than what Coolamon offered. I also knew that I didn't want to be a woman who messed up other women's lives.

'Stop,' I'd called, running after the pram. 'I'm sorry. I don't want this. I'm really, really sorry.'

She looked at me, the tears running down her cheeks. 'Come on,' she said to the little one, her eyes still on my face. 'Let's go home.'

There was a hollow in my body the rest of the day as I swept the cool, deep veranda and paths, dead-headed the roses, and weeded Mama's higgledy-piggledy collection of withering geraniums that she'd poked into rusty tins. But I knew what I had to do.

When Billy rang at the end of the day, his voice was warm, expectant. 'Hey, how are you?'

I steeled myself. 'We can't see each other again, Billy. I'm leaving in the morning.'

'You don't need to do that,' he said. 'It'll work out.'

But here I was, watching the paddocks of Paterson's Curse blur through my tears. I didn't know when I would go back to Coolamon again, whether I would see him again. There was no more fluttering or lurching in my body: I just felt sad. Marilyn French hadn't promised that change would come without tears but I hadn't been prepared for the intensity of the grief I felt.

I'd sent my mother a copy of *The Women's Room*, an enthusiastic misjudgement on my part. I'd thought she would relate to the drudgery of being a housewife: cooking, cleaning, washing, ironing, making ends meet, while Dad drank away their meagre income at the bowling club. I thought she would see that women had other options. I'd thought we could be excited together, but she didn't read past the second page, where there was a description of Mira being confronted by words on a toilet wall at the university: the graffiti included 'fuck' and 'cunt'.

'Don't bother sending me such trash again,' she'd written. 'I don't know what you were thinking. I'm not interested in your women's lib rubbish. If that's what it's about, I think it's disgusting. It's time you woke up to yourself.'

And maybe, finally, I was waking up to myself, not that I would ever tell her that.

As the train chugged past a deserted platform where the wheat silos bulged with the summer harvest, I thought about how all I'd ever wanted was for my mother to love me just as I was. I wondered if she was ever going to change. The night I'd led her back into the kitchen at Christmas, I'd felt an inkling of change in me: I'd discovered that I could survive her tears, her outrage – but I also resolved to be more careful sharing any memories with her in future.

In the distance, a haystack rising above the stubble resembled the farmers' homes that stood primped and preened at the end of long dusty driveways. I was seeing the world I'd grown up in with new eyes since coming back to Australia. I was waking up in lots of different ways. What I'd thought was boring and tedious was now marvellous. The straw-gold crops spreading into the distance perfectly complemented the blue of the midday sky, and the occasional puff of cloud was like the fresh white buttons on my favourite teenage dress, the crisp blue and white one with the dog-eared white collar. Even the brown splotches of sheep looked good, merging as they did with the muted grey-green gums they sheltered beneath. My chest had fluttered when I'd seen the red roofs of Sydney again, but it was the gum trees everywhere that really made my heart thump. Like the dead trunk reaching for the sky that I'd passed every day in the school bus, they triggered a yearning ache in my chest. But they made me smile too.

'The gum trees! Every one of them is different,' I'd gushed to Robin, as we drove the leafy Princes highway to Huskisson. 'They're just like people.'

'They're eucalypts, Di, not gum trees,' he'd chided.

'I don't care,' I'd replied. 'Gums. Eucalypts. I love them whatever they're called.'

The brakes screeched as the train slowed to a stop at Yass Junction. The carriage lights seemed very bright and it took me a moment or two to realise this part of my journey was at an end. As I pulled my bag down from the overhead rack, I noticed a stand of tall, sturdy eucalypts in a paddock across the rails. The bus to Canberra was waiting. I straightened my back, opened the door and took a deep breath.

Acknowledgements

I was privileged to be born on the country of the Wiradjuri people, and would like to acknowledge their sovereignty, which has never been ceded. I grew up on stolen Aboriginal land. I am pleased that their connection and custodianship is better recognised by many of the area's governing bodies in 2021 than it was when I was growing up. I acknowledge that the long denial, and worse, by my family and others who settled in that area, must have caused much distress. I am sorry, and I commit to continued learning about racism and endeavouring to live an anti-racist life.

I wrote this memoir on the lands of the Ngunnawal and Ngambri people and pay my respects to their elders, past and present, and thank them for their continuing generosity to us who live here, and their care for this beautiful place.

Coolamon Girl has been a long time in the writing and I want to thank my writing group who have walked alongside me on this journey offering loving, robust, and consistent advice and feedback. There's no way I would have arrived at this point without them. Thank you to Biff Ward, Robyn Cadwallader, Jenni Savigny, Karen Viggers and Jenny Shapcott (we miss you).

To Nicola O'Shea, who met with me at the Jugiong Writer's Festival in 2015 and offered much encouragement and her business card for future use, thank you. Your feedback, advice and editing helped me get this far in in the process.

Thank you to Helen, Jess and Bluse, for your early reading and support, and for your ongoing love.

Thank you to Helen, Johnny, Chris, Les and Noel (rest in peace), for your generosity in letting me write my version of our stories.

To all my Coolamon and Wagga schoolfriends who were happy to appear in the story, I love that we still know each other.

Thank you, kids (you know who you are), for your enthusiastic support and encouragement, and for not batting an eye at some of the cringe-worthy experiences of my younger self. You have made me who I am today.

Thank you, Pen Tayler, for your reading and the time you took to help me sort out a cover. Your photographic and technical skills are incredible.

Finally, thanks to Stephen at Ginninderra Press for his relaxed, quiet and supportive facilitation of the publishing process. It seems appropriate that *Coolamon Girl* is being brought to life by a publisher which we Canberrans proudly claim as our own.

www.ingramcontent.com/pod-product-compliance
Lightning Source LLC
Chambersburg PA
CBHW030905080526
44589CB00010B/156